Microsoft SQL Server 2012 with Hadoop

Integrate data between Apache Hadoop and SQL Server 2012 and provide business intelligence on the heterogeneous data

Debarchan Sarkar

BIRMINGHAM - MUMBAI

Microsoft SQL Server 2012 with Hadoop

First published: August 2013

Production Reference: 1200813

Published by Packt Publishing Ltd.
Livery Place
35 Livery Street
Birmingham B3 2PB, UK.

ISBN 978-1-78217-798-2

www.packtpub.com

Cover Image by Aniket Sawant (aniket_sawant_photography@hotmail.com)

Credits

Authors
Debarchan Sarkar

Reviewer
Atdhe Buja Msc

Acquisition Editor
James Jones

Commissioning Editor
Shaon Basu

Technical Editor
Chandni Maishery

Project Coordinator
Akash Poojary

Proofreader
Mario Cecere

Indexer
Rekha Nair

Tejal Soni

Graphics
Abhinash Sahu

Production Coordinator
Nilesh R. Mohite

Cover Work
Nilesh R. Mohite

About the Author

Debarchan Sarkar is a Microsoft Data Platform engineer who hails from Calcutta, the "city of joy", India. He has been a seasoned SQL Server engineer with Microsoft, India for the last six years and has now started venturing into the open source world, specifically the Apache Hadoop framework. He is a SQL Server Business Intelligence specialist with subject matter expertise in SQL Server Integration Services.

Debarchan is currently working on another book with Apress on Microsoft's Hadoop distribution, HDInsight.

I would like to thank my parents, Devjani Sarkar and Asok Sarkar for their continuous support and encouragement behind this book.

About the Reviewer

Atdhe Buja Msc is a Certified Ethical Hacker, Database Administrator (MCITP, OCA11g) and a developer with good management skills. He is a DBA at Ministry of Public Administration, Pristina, RKS, where he also manages some projects of E-Governance and eight years' experience in SQL Server.

Atdhe is a regular columnist for UBT News, currently he holds a MSc. in Computer Science and Engineering, has a Bachelor in Management and Information and continues studies for a Bachelor degree in Political Science in UP.

Specialized and Certified in many technologies such as SQL Server 2000, 2005, 2008, 2008 R2, Oracle 11g, CEH-Ethical Hacker, Windows Server, MS Project, System Center Operation Manager, and Web Design.

His capabilities go beyond the above mentioned knowledge!

I thank my wife Donika Bajrami and my family Buja for all the encouragement and support.

www.PacktPub.com

Support files, eBooks, discount offers and more

You might want to visit www.PacktPub.com for support files and downloads related to your book.

Did you know that Packt offers eBook versions of every book published, with PDF and ePub files available? You can upgrade to the eBook version at www.PacktPub.com and as a print book customer, you are entitled to a discount on the eBook copy. Get in touch with us at service@packtpub.com for more details.

At www.PacktPub.com, you can also read a collection of free technical articles, sign up for a range of free newsletters and receive exclusive discounts and offers on Packt books and eBooks.

http://PacktLib.PacktPub.com

Do you need instant solutions to your IT questions? PacktLib is Packt's online digital book library. Here, you can access, read and search across Packt's entire library of books.

Why Subscribe?

- Fully searchable across every book published by Packt
- Copy and paste, print and bookmark content
- On demand and accessible via web browser

Free Access for Packt account holders

If you have an account with Packt at www.PacktPub.com, you can use this to access PacktLib today and view nine entirely free books. Simply use your login credentials for immediate access.

Instant Updates on New Packt Books

Get notified! Find out when new books are published by following @PacktEnterprise on Twitter, or the *Packt Enterprise* Facebook page.

Table of Contents

Preface

Data management needs have evolved from traditional relational storage to both relational and non-relational storage and a modern information management platform needs to support all types of data. To deliver insight on any data, you need a platform that provides a complete set of capabilities for data management across relational, non-relational, and streaming data while being able to seamlessly move data from one type to another and being able to monitor and manage all your data regardless of the type of data or data structure it is. Apache Hadoop is the widely accepted Big Data tool, similarly, when it comes to RDBMS, SQL Server 2012 is perhaps the most powerful, in-memory and dynamic data storage and management system. This book enables the reader to bridge the gap between Hadoop and SQL Server, in other words, between the non-relational and relational data management worlds. The book specifically focusses on the data integration and visualization solutions that are available with the rich Business Intelligence suite of SQL Server and their seamless communication with Apache Hadoop and Hive.

What this book covers

Chapter 1, Introduction to Big Data and Hadoop, introduces the reader to the Big Data and Hadoop world. This chapter explains the need for Big Data solutions, the current market trends, and enables the user to be a step ahead during the data explosion that is soon to happen.

Chapter 2, Using Sqoop – SQL Server Hadoop Connector, covers the open source Sqoop-based Hadoop Connector for Microsoft SQL Server. This chapter explains the basic Sqoop commands to import/export files to and from SQL Server and Hadoop.

Chapter 3, Using the Hive ODBC Driver, explains the ways to consume data from Hadoop and Hive using the Open Database Connectivity (ODBC) interface. This chapter shows you how to create an SQL Server Integration Services package to move data from Hadoop to SQL Server using the Hive ODBC driver.

Chapter 4, Creating a data model with SQL Server Analysis Services, illustrates how to consume data from Hadoop and Hive from SQL Server Analysis Services. The reader will learn to use the Hive ODBC driver to create a Linked Server from SQL to Hive and build an Analysis Services multidimensional model.

Chapter 5, Using Microsoft's Self-Service Business Intelligence Tools, introduces the reader to the rich set of self-service BI tools available with SQL Server 2012 BI suite. This chapter explains how to build powerful visualization on Hadoop data quickly and easily with a few mouse clicks.

What you need for this book

Following are the software prerequisites for running the samples in the book:

- Apache Hadoop 1.0 cluster with Hive 0.9 configured
- SQL Server 2012 with Integration Services and Analysis Services installed
- Microsoft Office 2013

Who this book is for

This book is for readers who are already familiar with Hadoop and its supporting technologies and are willing to cross pollinate their skills with Microsoft SQL Server 2012 Business Intelligence suite. The readers will learn how to integrate data between these two ecosystems to provide more meaningful insights while visualizing the data. This book also gives the reader a glimpse of the self-service BI tools available with SQL Server and Excel and how to leverage them to generate powerful visualization of data in a matter of few clicks.

Conventions

In this book, you will find a number of styles of text that distinguish between different kinds of information. Here are some examples of these styles, and an explanation of their meaning.

Code words in text, database table names, folder names, filenames, file extensions, pathnames, dummy URLs, user input, and Twitter handles are shown as follows: "NoSQL storage is typically much cheaper than relational storage, and usually supports a write-once capability that allows only for data to be appended."

Any command-line input or output is written as follows:

```
$bin/ sqoop import --connect
"jdbc:sqlserver://<YourServerName>;username=<user>;password=<pwd>;
database=Adventureworks2012" --table ErrorLog --target-dir
/data/ErrorLogs --as-textfile
```

New terms and **important words** are shown in bold. Words that you see on the screen, in menus or dialog boxes for example, appear in the text like this: "First, create a **System DSN**. In **ODBC Data Sources Administrator**, go to the **System DSN** tab and click on the **Add Button** as shown in the following screenshot".

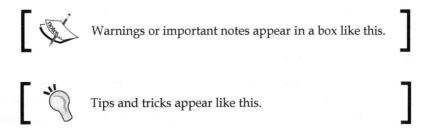

Warnings or important notes appear in a box like this.

Tips and tricks appear like this.

Reader feedback

Feedback from our readers is always welcome. Let us know what you think about this book — what you liked or may have disliked. Reader feedback is important for us to develop titles that you really get the most out of.

To send us general feedback, simply send an e-mail to feedback@packtpub.com, and mention the book title via the subject of your message.

If there is a topic that you have expertise in and you are interested in either writing or contributing to a book, see our author guide on www.packtpub.com/authors.

Customer support

Now that you are the proud owner of a Packt book, we have a number of things to help you to get the most from your purchase.

Errata

Although we have taken every care to ensure the accuracy of our content, mistakes do happen. If you find a mistake in one of our books—maybe a mistake in the text or the code—we would be grateful if you would report this to us. By doing so, you can save other readers from frustration and help us improve subsequent versions of this book. If you find any errata, please report them by visiting `http://www.packtpub.com/submit-errata`, selecting your book, clicking on the **errata submission form** link, and entering the details of your errata. Once your errata are verified, your submission will be accepted and the errata will be uploaded on our website, or added to any list of existing errata, under the Errata section of that title. Any existing errata can be viewed by selecting your title from `http://www.packtpub.com/support`.

Piracy

Piracy of copyright material on the Internet is an ongoing problem across all media. At Packt, we take the protection of our copyright and licenses very seriously. If you come across any illegal copies of our works, in any form, on the Internet, please provide us with the location address or website name immediately so that we can pursue a remedy.

Please contact us at `copyright@packtpub.com` with a link to the suspected pirated material.

We appreciate your help in protecting our authors, and our ability to bring you valuable content.

Questions

You can contact us at `questions@packtpub.com` if you are having a problem with any aspect of the book, and we will do our best to address it.

1
Introduction to Big Data and Hadoop

Suddenly, Big Data is the talk of the town. Every company ranging from enterprise-level to small-scale startups has money for Big Data. The storage and hardware costs have dramatically reduced over the past few years enabling the businesses to store and analyze data, which were earlier discarded due to storage and processing challenges. There has never been a more exciting time with respect to the world of data. We are seeing the convergence of significant trends that are fundamentally transforming the industry and a new era of tech innovation in areas such as social, mobile, advanced analytics, and machine learning. We're seeing an explosion of data where there is an entirely new scale and scope to the kinds of data we are trying to gain insights from. In this chapter, we will get an insight on what Big Data is and how the Apache Hadoop framework comes in the picture when implementing Big Data solutions. After reading through the chapter, you will be able to understand:

- What is Big Data and why now
- Business needs for Big Data
- The Apache Hadoop framework

Big Data – what's the big deal?

There's a lot of talk about Big Data—estimates are that the total amount of digital information in the world is increasing ten times every five years, with 85 percent of this data coming from new data types for example, sensors, RFIDs, web logs, and so on. This presents a huge opportunity for businesses that tap into this new data to identify new opportunity and areas for innovation.

However, having a platform that supports the data trend is only a part of today's challenge; you need to also make it easier for people to access so that they can gain insight and make better decisions. If you think about the user experience, with everything we are able to do on the Web, our experiences through social media sites, how we're discovering, sharing, and collaborating in new ways, user expectations of their business, and productivity applications are changing as well.

One of the first questions we should set out to answer is a simple definitional one: how is Big Data different from traditional large data warehouses? International Data Corporation has the most broadly accepted theory of classifying Big Data as the three Vs:

- **Volume**: Data volume is exploding. In the last few decades, computing and storage capacity have grown exponentially, driving down hardware and storage costs to near zero and making them a commodity. The current data processing needs are evolving and are demanding analysis of petabytes and zetabytes of data with industry standard hardware within minutes if not seconds.

- **Variety**: The variety of data is increasing. It's all getting stored and nearly 85 percent of new data is unstructured data. The data can be in the form of tweets, JSONs with variable attributes and elements of which users may want to process selective ones.

- **Velocity**: The velocity of data is speeding up the pace of business. Data capture has become nearly instantaneous, thanks to new customer interaction points and technologies. Real-time analytics is more important than ever. The ratio of data remittance rate continues to be way higher than the data consumption rate; coping with the speed of data continues to be a challenge. Think about a software that can let you message or type as fast as the speed of your thought.

Today, every organization finds it difficult to manage and track the right dataset within itself, the challenge is even greater when they need to look out for data which is external to the system. A typical analyst spends too much time searching for the right data from thousands of sources, which adversely impacts productivity. We will move from a world of search to one of discovery, where information is brought to the user based on who you are, and what you are working on. There has never been such an abundance of externally available and useful information as there is today. The challenge is how do you discover what is available and how do you connect to it?

To answer today's types of question, you need new ways to discover and explore data. By this we mean, data that may reside in a number of different domains such as:

- **Personal data**: This is data created by me, or by my peers, but relevant for the task at hand.

- **Organizational data**: This is data that is maintained and managed across the organization.

- **Community data**: This is external data such as curated third party datasets that are shared into the public domain. Examples include Data.gov, Twitter, Facebook, and so on.

- **World data**: This is all the other data that is available on the global stage, for example, data from sensors or logfiles, and for which technologies such as Hadoop for Big Data have emerged.

You could derive much deeper business insight and trends by combining the data you need across personal, corporate, community, and world data. You can connect and combine data from hundreds of trusted data providers — data includes demographic data, environment data, financial data, retail and sports data, social data such as twitter and facebook as well as data cleansing services. You can combine this data with your personal data through self-service tools, for example, PowerPivot, you can use reference data for cleansing your corporate data with SQL Server 2012, or you can use it in your custom applications.

Existing RDBMS solutions as SQL Server are good in managing challenging volumes of data, but it falls short when the data is unstructured or semi-structured with variable attributes such as the ones discussed previously. The current world seems almost obsessed with social media sentiments, tweets, devices, and so on; without the right tools, your company is adrift in a sea of data. You need the ability to unleash the wave of new value made possible by Big Data. It's all and every bit of data that you should be able to easily monitor and manage regardless of type or structure. That's why organizations are trending to build an end-to-end data platform for nearly all data and easy-to-use tools to analyze it. Regardless of data type, location (on-premises or in the cloud), or size, you have the power of familiar tools coupled with high-performance technologies to serve your business needs from data storage, processing, and all the way to visualization. The benefits of Big Data are not limited only to **Business Intelligence** (**BI**) experts or data scientists. Nearly everyone in your organization can analyze and make more informed decisions with the right tools.

In a traditional business environment, the data to power your reporting mechanism will usually come from tables in a database. However, it's increasingly necessary to supplement this with data obtained from outside your organization. This may be commercially available datasets, such as those available from Windows Data Market and elsewhere, or it may be data from less structured sources such as feeds, e-mails, logfiles, and more. You will, in most cases, need to cleanse, validate, and transform this data before loading it into an existing database. **Extract, Transform, and Load (ETL)** operations can use Big Data solutions to perform pattern matching, data categorization, deduplication, and summary operations on unstructured or semi-structured data to generate data in the familiar rows and columns format that can be imported into a database table. The following figure will give you a conceptual view of Big Data:

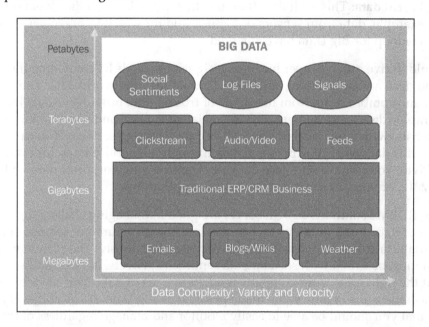

Big Data requires some level of machine learning or complex statistical processing to produce insights. If you have to use non-standard techniques to process and host it; it's probably Big Data.

The data store in a Big Data implementation is usually referred to as a NoSQL store, although this is not technically accurate because some implementations do support a SQL-like query language. NoSQL storage is typically much cheaper than relational storage, and usually supports a write-once capability that allows only for data to be appended. To update data in these stores you must drop and recreate the relevant file. This limitation maximizes performance; Big Data storage implementations are usually measured by throughput rather than capacity because this is usually the most significant factor for both storage and query efficiency. This approach also provides better performance and maintains the history of changes to the data.

 However, it is extremely important to note that, in addition to supporting all types of data, moving data to and from a non-relational store such as Hadoop and a relational data warehouse such as SQL Server is one of the key Big Data customer usage patterns. Throughout this book, we will explore how we can integrate Hadoop and SQL Server and derive powerful visualization on any data using the SQL Server BI suite.

The Apache Hadoop framework

Hadoop is an open source software framework that supports data-intensive distributed applications available through the Apache Open Source community. It consists of a distributed file system **HDFS**, the **Hadoop Distributed File System** and an approach to distributed processing of analysis called MapReduce. It is written in Java and based on the Linux/Unix platform.

It's used (extensively now) in the processing of streams of data that go well beyond even the largest enterprise datasets in size. Whether it's sensor, clickstream, social media, location-based, or other data that is generated and collected in large gobs, Hadoop is often on the scene in the service of processing and analyzing it. The real magic of Hadoop is its ability to move the processing or computing logic to the data where it resides as opposed to traditional systems, which focus on a scaled-up single server, move the data to that central processing unit and process the data there. This model does not work on the volume, velocity, and variety of data that present day industry is looking to mine for business intelligence. Hence, Hadoop with its powerful fault tolerant and reliable file system and highly optimized distributed computing model, is one of the leaders in the Big Data world.

The core of Hadoop is its storage system and its distributed computing model:

HDFS

Hadoop Distributed File System is a program level abstraction on top of the host OS file system. It is responsible for storing data on the cluster. Data is split into blocks and distributed across multiple nodes in the cluster.

MapReduce

MapReduce is a programming model for processing large datasets using distributed computing on clusters of computers. MapReduce consists of two phases: dividing the data across a large number of separate processing units (called Map), and then combining the results produced by these individual processes into a unified result set (called Reduce). Between Map and Reduce, shuffle and sort occur. Hadoop cluster, once successfully configured on a system, has the following basic components:

NameNode

This is also called the Head Node/Master Node of the cluster. Primarily, it holds the metadata for HDFS during processing of data which is distributed across the nodes; it keeps track of each HDFS data block in the nodes.

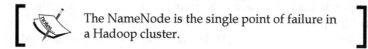

> The NameNode is the single point of failure in a Hadoop cluster.

Secondary NameNode

This is an optional node that you can have in your cluster to back up the NameNode if it goes down. If a secondary NameNode is configured, it keeps a periodic snapshot of the NameNode configuration to serve as a backup when needed. However, there is no automated way for failing over to the secondary NameNode; if the primary NameNode goes down, a manual intervention is needed. This essentially means that there would be an obvious down time in your cluster in case the NameNode goes down.

DataNode

These are the systems across the cluster which store the actual HDFS data blocks. The data blocks are replicated on multiple nodes to provide fault tolerant and high availability solutions.

JobTracker

This is a service running on the NameNode, which manages MapReduce jobs and distributes individual tasks.

TaskTracker

This is a service running on the DataNodes, which instantiates and monitors individual Map and Reduce tasks that are submitted.

The following figure shows you the core components of the Apache Hadoop framework:

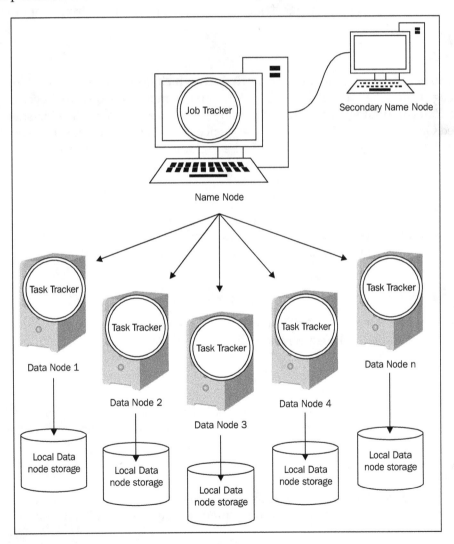

Additionally, there are a number of supporting projects for Hadoop, each having their unique purpose for example, to feed input data to Hadoop system, a data warehousing system for ad hoc queries on top of Hadoop, and many more. The following are a few worth mentioning:

Hive

Hive is a supporting project for the main Apache Hadoop project and is an abstraction on top of MapReduce, which allows users to query the data without developing MapReduce applications. It provides the user with a SQL-like query language called **Hive Query Language (HQL)** to fetch data from Hive store. This makes it easier for people with SQL skills to adapt to Hadoop environment quickly.

Pig

Pig is an alternative abstraction on MapReduce, which uses dataflow scripting language called PigLatin. This is favored by programmers who already have scripting skills. You can run PigLatin statements interactively in a command line Pig shell named Grunt. You can also combine a sequence of PigLatin statements in a script, which can then be executed as a unit. These PigLatin statements are used to generate MapReduce jobs by the Pig interpreter and are executed on the HDFS data.

Flume

Flume is another open source implementation on top of Hadoop, which provides a data-ingestion mechanism for data into HDFS as data is generated.

Sqoop

Sqoop provides a way to import and export data to and from relational database tables (for example, SQL Server) and HDFS.

Oozie

Oozie allows creation of workflow of MapReduce jobs. This is familiar with developers who have worked on Workflow and communication foundation based solutions.

HBase

HBase is Hadoop database, a NoSQL database. It is another abstraction on top of Hadoop, which provides a near real-time query mechanisms to HDFS data.

Mahout

Mahout is a machine-learning library that contains algorithms for clustering and classification. One major focus of machine-learning research is to automatically learn to recognize complex patterns and make intelligent decisions based on data.

The following figure gives you a 1000 feet view of the Apache Hadoop and the various supporting projects that form this amazing ecosystem:

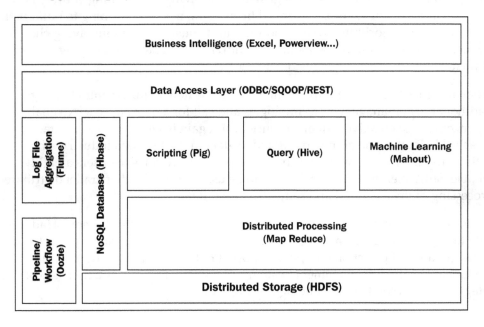

We will be exploring some of these components in the subsequent chapters of this book, but for a complete reference, please visit the Apache website `http://hadoop.apache.org/`.

Setting up this ecosystem along with the required supporting projects could be really non-trivial. In fact the only drawback this implementation has, is the effort needed to set up and administer a Hadoop cluster. This is basically the reason that many vendors are coming up with their own distribution of Hadoop bundled and distributed as a data processing platform. Using these distributions, enterprises would be able to set up Hadoop clusters in minutes through simplified and user-friendly cluster deployment wizards and also use the various dashboards for monitoring and instrumentation purposes. Some of the present day distributions are *CH4 from Cloudera, Hortonworks Data Platform*, and *Microsoft HDInsight*, which are quickly gaining popularity. These distributions are outside the scope of this book and won't be covered; please visit the respective websites for detailed information about these distributions.

Summary

In this chapter, we went through what Big Data is and why it is one of the compelling needs of the industry. The diversity of data that needs to be processed has taken Information Technology to heights that were never imagined before. Organizations that are able to take advantage of Big Data to parse any and every data will be able to more effectively differentiate and derive new value for the business, whether it is in the form of revenue growth, cost savings, or creating entirely new business models. For example, financial firms using machine learning to build better fraud detection algorithms, go beyond the simple business rules involving charge frequency and location to also include an individual's customized buying patterns ultimately leading to a better customer experience.

When it comes to Big Data implementations, these new requirements challenge traditional data management technologies and call for a new approach to enable organizations to effectively manage, enrich, and gain insights from any data. Apache Hadoop is one of the undoubted leaders in the Big Data industry. The entire ecosystem, along with its supporting projects provides the users a highly reliable, fault tolerant framework that can be used for massively parallel distributed processing of unstructured and semi-structured data.

In the next chapter, you will see how to use the Sqoop connector to move Hadoop data to SQL Server 2012 and vice versa. Sqoop is another open source project, which is designed for bi-directional import/export of data from Hadoop from/to any Relational Database Management System; we will see its usage as a first step of data integration between Hadoop and SQL Server 2012.

2

Using Sqoop – The SQL Server Hadoop Connector

Sqoop is an open source Apache project, which facilitates data exchange between Hadoop and any traditional **Relational Database Management System (RDBMS)**. It uses the MapReduce framework under the hood to perform the import/export operations and often is a common choice for integrating data from relational and non-relational data stores.

Microsoft SQL Server Connector for Apache Hadoop (SQL Server-Hadoop Connector) is a Sqoop-based connector that is specifically designed for efficient data transfer between SQL Server and Hadoop. This connector is optimized for bulk transfer of the data bi-directionally, it does not support extensive formatting or transformation on the data while being imported or exported on the fly. After reading this chapter, you will be able to:

- Install and configure the Sqoop connector
- Import data from SQL Server to Hadoop
- Export data from Hadoop to SQL Server

The SQL Server-Hadoop Connector

Sqoop is implemented using JDBC and so it also conforms to the standard JDBC features. The schema or the structure of the data is provided by the data source, and Sqoop generates and executes SQL statements using JDBC. The following table summarizes a few important commands that are available with the SQL Server connector and their functionalities:

Command	Function
sqoop import	The import command lets you import SQL Server data into HDFS. You can opt to import an entire table using the --table switch or selected records based on criteria using the --query switch. The data, once imported to the Hadoop file system, are stored as delimited text files or as SequenceFiles for further processing. You can also use the import command to move SQL Server data into Hive tables, which are like logical schemas on top of HDFS.
sqoop export	You can use the export command to move data from HDFS into SQL Server tables. Much like the import command, the export command lets you export data from delimited text files, SequenceFiles, and Hive tables into SQL Server. The export command supports inserting new rows to the target SQL Server table, update existing rows based on an update key column as well as invoking a stored procedure execution.
sqoop job	The job command enables you to save your import/export commands as a job for future reuse. The saved jobs remember the parameters that are specified during execution and particularly useful when there is a need to run an import/export command repeatedly on a periodic basis.
sqoop version	To quickly check the version of sqoop you are on, you can run the sqoop version command to print the installed version details in the console.

The SequenceFiles in Hadoop are binary content that contain serialized data as opposed to delimited text files. Please refer to the Hadoop page http://hadoop.apache.org/docs/current/api/org/apache/hadoop/io/SequenceFile.html for a detailed understanding on how SequenceFiles are structured. Also, we would go through a few sample import/export commands with different arguments in the subsequent sections of this chapter. Please refer to the Apache Sqoop user guide http://sqoop.apache.org/docs/1.4.2/SqoopUserGuide.html for a complete reference on Sqoop commands and their switches.

 Hive is a data warehouse infrastructure built on top of Hadoop, which is discussed in the next chapter.

Installation prerequisites

This chapter assumes that you have a Linux cluster with Hadoop and Hive configured and a Windows system with SQL Server 2012 running on it. Both of these environments are required to use the SQL Server-Hadoop Connector and to run the sample commands in this chapter.

A Hadoop cluster on Linux

The first step is to have a Hadoop cluster up and running on Linux. We will use this cluster's HDFS to import and export data from SQL Server. The sample commands in this chapter assume that they are run on Hadoop Version 1.1.0, Hive Version 0.9.0 on Red Hat Enterprise Linux 5.8.

 Make sure that the HADOOP_HOME environment variable is set to the parent directory, where Hadoop is installed.

Installing and configuring Sqoop

The next step is to install and configure the Sqoop connector, if not already installed, on the NameNode of your Hadoop cluster. I recommend downloading and installing Sqoop 1.4.2 from Apache's website, which is the version used to run the sample commands in this chapter.

After the installation is done, you must verify whether the Sqoop environment variables are set with proper values. They should be set to point to the path as described in the following table for the SQL Server-Hadoop Connector to function correctly. This also relieves you from fully qualifying the path of the various Sqoop command-line utilities each time you need to execute them.

The following table describes Sqoop environment variables:

Environment Variable	Value to Assign
SQOOP_HOME	Absolute path where you have installed Sqoop.
SQOOP_CONF_DIR	$SQOOP_HOME/conf assuming that SQOOP_HOME already has the correct value set.

Setting up the Microsoft JDBC driver

Sqoop and SQL Server-Hadoop Connector uses **Java Database Connectivity (JDBC)** technology to establish connections to remote RDBMS servers and therefore needs the JDBC driver for SQL Server. This chapter assumes the usage of the SQL Server JDBC driver Version 3.0 (sqljdbc_3.0). To install this driver on the Linux NameNode, where you have just installed Sqoop, perform the following steps:

1. Visit `http://www.microsoft.com/en-us/download/details.aspx?displaylang=en&id=21599` and download `sqljdbc_3.0_enu.tar.gz` to the NameNode of your cluster.

2. Use the following command to unpack the downloaded file: `tar -zxvf sqljdbc_3.0_enu.tar.gz`. This will create a directory `sqljdbc_3.0` in current directory.

3. Copy the driver jar (`sqljdbc_3.0/enu/sqljdbc4.jar`) file to the `$SQOOP_HOME/lib` directory on the NameNode.

Downloading the SQL Server-Hadoop Connector

If you have reached this point, finally, you are ready to download, install, and configure the SQL Server-Hadoop Connector on the NameNode of your cluster.

The Microsoft SQL Server SQOOP Connector for Hadoop is now part of Apache SQOOP 1.4.x series of projects, and Microsoft no longer provides a separate download from their site. The connector is now downloadable from Apache's website: `http://sqoop.apache.org/`

The following table summarizes the different files that are deployed to the NameNode once the connector is downloaded. The table contains the SQL Server-Hadoop Connector installer archive:

File/Directory	Description
`install.sh`	This is a shell script that has commands to copy the necessary files and directory structure for the SQL Server-Hadoop Connector.
`Microsoft SQL Server-Hadoop Connector User Guide.pdf`	User guide to deploy and execute SQL Server-Hadoop Connector commands.

File/Directory	Description
`lib/`	This directory contains the `sqoop-sqlserver-1.0.jar` file. This is the archive that has most of the Sqoop command definitions.
`conf/`	This directory contains the configuration files for SQL Server-Hadoop Connector.
`THIRDPARTYNOTICES FOR HADOOP-BASED CONNECTORS.txt`	This document consists of the third party notices.
`SQL Server Connector for Apache Hadoop MSLT.pdf`	End User License Agreement for the SQL Server Connector for Apache Hadoop.

Installing the SQL Server-Hadoop Connector

The following steps need to be performed in order to install SQL Server-Hadoop Connector:

1. Log in to your cluster NameNode using a user credential, which has the permission to install files.
2. Extract the archive with the command: `tar -zxvf sqoop-sqlserver-1.0.tar.gz`. This will create `sqoop-sqlserver-1.0` directory in the present working directory.
3. Ensure that the `MSSQL_CONNECTOR_HOME` environment variable is set to the absolute path of the `sqoop-sqlserver-1.0` directory.
4. Change directory (`cd`) to the `sqoop-sqlserver-1.0` and run the shell `scriptinstall.sh` without any additional arguments.
5. Installer will copy the connector jar and configuration files under existing Sqoop installation directory.

The Sqoop import tool

You're now ready to use SQL Server-Hadoop Connector and import data from SQL Server 2012 to HDFS. The input to the import process is a SQL Server table, which will be read row-by-row into HDFS by Sqoop. The output of this import process is a set of files containing a copy of the imported table. Since the import process is performed in parallel, the output will be in multiple files.

When using the sqoop import command, you must specify the following mandatory arguments:

- --connect argument specifying the connection string to the SQL Server database

- --username and --password arguments to provide valid credentials to connect to the SQL Server database

- --table or --query argument to import an entire table or results of a custom query execution

The following command imports data from ErrorLog table in SQL Server Adventureworks2012 database to delimited text files in /data/ErrorLogs directory on HDFS.

> Sqoop 1.4.2 does not recognize SQL Server tables, which do not belong to the default dbo schema. This is fixed with the addition of the --schema switch, where you can specify non-default schema names in Sqoop 1.4.3.

The following command describes how to import data to HDFS from SQL Server table:

```
$bin/ sqoop import --connect
  "jdbc:sqlserver://<YourServerName>;username=<user>;password=<pwd>;
  database=Adventureworks2012" --table ErrorLog --target-dir
  /data/ErrorLogs --as-textfile
```

> You can also use --as-avrodatafile or --as-sequencefile to import the data to Avro files and SequenceFiles respectively as opposed to plain text when using --as-textfile in the previous sample command.

Successful execution of the previous code will transfer all the records of the SQL table to a comma delimited HDFS file and the output should resemble the following screenshot:

```
C:\Hadoop\sqoop-1.4.2\bin>sqoop import --connect "jdbc:sqlserver://       ;userna
me=   ;password=   ;database=AdventureWorks2008R2" --table ErrorLog --target-dir /
data/ErrorLogs
Setting HBASE_HOME to
Warning: HBASE_HOME [c:\hadoop\hadoop-1.1.0-SNAPSHOT\hbase-0.94.2] does not exis
t HBase imports will fail.
Please set HBASE_HOME to the root of your HBase installation.
Setting ZOOKEEPER_HOME to
Warning: ZOOKEEPER_HOME [c:\hadoop\hadoop-1.1.0-SNAPSHOT\zookeeper-3.4.3] does n
ot exist
Please set $ZOOKEEPER_HOME to the root of your Zookeeper installation.
13/05/13 13:35:23 INFO manager.SqlManager: Using default fetchSize of 1000
13/05/13 13:35:23 INFO tool.CodeGenTool: Beginning code generation
13/05/13 13:35:23 INFO manager.SqlManager: Executing SQL statement: SELECT t.* F
ROM [ErrorLog] AS t WHERE 1=0
13/05/13 13:35:23 INFO orm.CompilationManager: HADOOP_HOME is c:\Hadoop\hadoop-1
.1.0-SNAPSHOT
Note: \tmp\sqoop-desarkar\compile\9ad7576ae175a0ab1479dc44df691dbb\ErrorLog.java
 uses or overrides a deprecated API.
Note: Recompile with -Xlint:deprecation for details.
13/05/13 13:35:24 INFO orm.CompilationManager: Writing jar file: \tmp\sqoop-desa
rkar\compile\9ad7576ae175a0ab1479dc44df691dbb\ErrorLog.jar
13/05/13 13:35:24 INFO mapreduce.ImportJobBase: Beginning import of ErrorLog
13/05/13 13:35:25 INFO db.DataDrivenDBInputFormat: BoundingValsQuery: SELECT MIN
([ErrorLogID]), MAX([ErrorLogID]) FROM [ErrorLog]
13/05/13 13:35:25 INFO mapred.JobClient: Running job: job_201304221124_0003
13/05/13 13:35:26 INFO mapred.JobClient:  map 0% reduce 0%
13/05/13 13:36:03 INFO mapred.JobClient:  map 100% reduce 0%
13/05/13 13:36:09 INFO mapred.JobClient: Job complete: job_201304221124_0003
13/05/13 13:36:09 INFO mapred.JobClient: Counters: 17
13/05/13 13:36:09 INFO mapred.JobClient:   Job Counters
13/05/13 13:36:09 INFO mapred.JobClient:     SLOTS_MILLIS_MAPS=12256
13/05/13 13:36:09 INFO mapred.JobClient:     Total time spent by all reduces wai
ting after reserving slots (ms)=0
13/05/13 13:36:09 INFO mapred.JobClient:     Total time spent by all maps waitin
g after reserving slots (ms)=0
13/05/13 13:36:09 INFO mapred.JobClient:     Launched map tasks=1
13/05/13 13:36:09 INFO mapred.JobClient:     SLOTS_MILLIS_REDUCES=0
13/05/13 13:36:09 INFO mapred.JobClient:   File Output Format Counters
13/05/13 13:36:09 INFO mapred.JobClient:     Bytes Written=0
13/05/13 13:36:09 INFO mapred.JobClient:   FileSystemCounters
13/05/13 13:36:09 INFO mapred.JobClient:     HDFS_BYTES_READ=121
13/05/13 13:36:09 INFO mapred.JobClient:     FILE_BYTES_WRITTEN=34307
13/05/13 13:36:09 INFO mapred.JobClient:   File Input Format Counters
13/05/13 13:36:09 INFO mapred.JobClient:     Bytes Read=0
13/05/13 13:36:09 INFO mapred.JobClient:   Map-Reduce Framework
13/05/13 13:36:09 INFO mapred.JobClient:     Map input records=0
13/05/13 13:36:09 INFO mapred.JobClient:     Physical memory (bytes) snapshot=10
3239680
13/05/13 13:36:09 INFO mapred.JobClient:     Spilled Records=0
13/05/13 13:36:09 INFO mapred.JobClient:     CPU time spent (ms)=623
13/05/13 13:36:09 INFO mapred.JobClient:     Total committed heap usage (bytes)=
128057344
13/05/13 13:36:09 INFO mapred.JobClient:     Virtual memory (bytes) snapshot=204
582912
```

You can specify a --split-by argument to the sqoop import command and specify a column to determine how the data is split between the mappers. If you do not specify a split-by column, then, by default, the primary key column is used. The following command specifies split-by column to compute the splits for mappers:

```
$bin/sqoop import --connect
  "jdbc:sqlserver://<YourServerName>;username=<user>;
  password=<pwd>;database=Adventureworks2012" --table ErrorLog --
  target-dir /data/ErrorLogsSplitBy --split-by  ErrorLogID -m  3
```

Importing the tables in Hive

Sqoop provides you with -hive-import argument to import a SQL Server table directly into a Hive table. The following command shows how to import SQL Server data to Hive:

```
$bin/ sqoop import --connect
  "jdbc:sqlserver://<YourServerName>;username=<user>;password=<pwd>;
  database=Adventureworks2012" --table ErrorLog -hive-import
```

Note the difference in the last section of the command line output, which confirms the operation in Hive as shown in the following screenshot:

```
13/05/13 14:10:15 INFO mapred.JobClient:      Map output records=0
13/05/13 14:10:15 INFO mapred.JobClient:      SPLIT_RAW_BYTES=121
13/05/13 14:10:15 INFO mapreduce.ImportJobBase: Transferred 0 bytes in 38.5898
econds (0 bytes/sec)
13/05/13 14:10:15 INFO mapreduce.ImportJobBase: Retrieved 0 records.
13/05/13 14:10:15 INFO manager.SqlManager: Executing SQL statement: SELECT t.*
ROM [ErrorLog] AS  t WHERE 1=0
13/05/13 14:10:15 WARN hive.TableDefWriter: Column ErrorTime had to be cast to
 less precise type in Hive
13/05/13 14:10:15 INFO hive.HiveImport: Removing temporary files from import pr
cess: hdfs://localhost:8020/user/desarkar/ErrorLog/_logs
13/05/13 14:10:15 INFO hive.HiveImport: Loading uploaded data into Hive
13/05/13 14:10:17 INFO hive.HiveImport: Logging initialized using configuration
in file:/C:/Hadoop/hive-0.9.0/conf/hive-log4j.properties
13/05/13 14:10:17 INFO hive.HiveImport: log4j:ERROR Failed to rename [c:\hadoop
hive-0.9.0\logs/hive.log] to [c:\hadoop\hive-0.9.0\logs/hive.log.2013-04-22].
13/05/13 14:10:17 INFO hive.HiveImport: Hive history file=c:\hadoop\hive-0.9.0\
ogs\history/hive_job_log_desarkar_201305131410_452002360.txt
13/05/13 14:10:26 INFO hive.HiveImport: OK
13/05/13 14:10:26 INFO hive.HiveImport: Time taken: 8.088 seconds
13/05/13 14:10:26 INFO hive.HiveImport: Loading data to table default.errorlog
13/05/13 14:10:26 INFO hive.HiveImport: OK
13/05/13 14:10:26 INFO hive.HiveImport: Time taken: 0.251 seconds
13/05/13 14:10:26 INFO hive.HiveImport: Hive import complete.
```

> For using Hive import command, ensure that Hive is installed and HIVE_HOME is set to the parent directory, where Hive is installed.

After running the `import` commands, you can verify the output folders created in your Hadoop NameNode admin portal as shown in the following screenshot:

Goto : /data [go]

Go to parent directory

Name	Type	Size	Replication	Block Size	Modification Time	Permission	Owner	Group
AdventureWorksCustomerData	dir				2013-05-13 13:30	rwxr-xr-x	desarkar	supergroup
ErrorLogs	dir				2013-05-13 13:36	rwxr-xr-x	desarkar	supergroup
ErrorLogsSequence	dir				2013-05-13 14:07	rwxr-xr-x	desarkar	supergroup
ErrorLogsSpliBy	dir				2013-05-13 14:05	rwxr-xr-x	desarkar	supergroup
SurveyData	dir				2013-05-13 13:11	rwxr-xr-x	desarkar	supergroup

Go back to DFS home

The Sqoop export tool

As stated earlier, Sqoop is a bi-directional connector. Sqoop's export process will read a set of delimited text files from HDFS in parallel, parse them into records, and insert them as new rows in a target database table. The following examples export data from HDFS and Hive to SQL Server. The assumption is that you are running the commands from the `$SQOOP_HOME` directory on the master node of the Hadoop cluster, where Sqoop is installed.

When using the `sqoop export` command, you must specify the following mandatory arguments:

- `--connect` argument specifying the connection string to the SQL Server database
- `--username` and `--password` arguments to provide valid credentials to connect to the SQL Server database
- `--table` or `--call` argument to export to an SQL table or invoke a stored procedure call
- `--export-dir` argument to specify the HDFS directory to export

The following command exports data back from a delimited text file in `/data/ErrorLogs` on HDFS to `ErrorLog` table in `Adventureworks2012` database on SQL Server:

```
$bin/ sqoop export --connect
  "jdbc:sqlserver://<YourServerName>;username=<user>;password=<pwd>;
  database=Adventureworks2012" --table ErrorLog-export-dir
  /data/ErrorLogs
```

You can specify the number of mappers while executing your `export` command.

The following command exports data from a delimited text file on HDFS with user defined number of map tasks:

```
$bin/sqoop export --connect
  "jdbc:sqlserver://<YourServerName>;username=<user>;password=<pwd>;
  database=Adventureworks2012" --table ErrorLog-export-dir
  /data/ErrorLogs-m 3
```

It is often a practice to use Sqoop to host data in an intermediate staging table to apply some transform and business logic before finally loading the data into the warehouse. The following command uses a staging table and specifies to first clear the staging table before starting the export:

```
$bin/sqoop export --connect
  "jdbc:sqlserver://<YourServerName>;username=<user>;password=<pwd>;
  database=Adventureworks2012"    --table ErrorLog
  --export-dir /data/ErrorLogs--staging-table ErrorLog_stage --clear-
  staging-table
```

 For current release, using `--direct` option has nothing to do with execution of `import`/`export` flow.

Data types

The following table summarizes the data types supported by this version of the SQL Server-Hadoop Connector. You should refer to this guide to avoid any type of compatibility issue during or after migration of data. All other native SQL Server types for example XML, geography, geometry, sql_variant, and so on, which are not mentioned in the following table are not supported as of now:

Data type category	SQL Server data type	SQL Server data type range	Sqoop data type	Sqoop data type range
Exact numeric	bigint	-2^{63} to $2^{63}-1$	Long	Max_value: $2^{63}-1$ (9223372036854775807) Min_value: -2^{63} (9223372036854775808)
	bit	0 or 1	Boolean	1-bit

Data type category	SQL Server data type	SQL Server data type range	Sqoop data type	Sqoop data type range
	int	-2^31 to 2^31-1	Integer	Max_value: 2^31-1 (2147483647) Min_value: -2^31 (-2147483648)
Approximate numeric	float	- 1.79E+308 to -2.23E-308, 0 and 2.23E-308 to 1.79E+308	Double	Max_value: (2-2^52) ·2^1023 or (1.7976931348623157E308d) Min_value: 2^-1074 or (4.9E-324d)
Date and time	date	January 1, 1 A.D. through December 31, 9999 A.D	java.sql. Date	int year, int month, int date: year: the year minus 1900. Must be 0 to 8099(Note that 8099 is 9999 minus 1900) month: 0 to 11 day: 1 to 31
	datetime	Date Range: January 1, 1753, through December 31, 9999 Time Range: 00:00:00 through 23:59:59.997	java.sql. Timestamp	int year, int month, int date, int hour, int minute, int second, intnano: year: the year minus 1900 month: 0 to 11 date: 1 to 31 hour: 0 to 23 minute: 0 to 59 second: 0 to 59 nano: 0 to 999,999,999

Data type category	SQL Server data type	SQL Server data type range	Sqoop data type	Sqoop data type range
Character strings	char	Fixed-length, non-Unicode character data	String	Up to 8,000 characters
		With a length of n bytes. n must be a value from 1 through 8,000.		
	varchar	Variable-length, non-Unicode character data. n can be a value from 1 through 8,000.	String	Up to 8,000 characters
		Varchar (max) is not supported.		
Unicode character strings	nchar	Fixed-length Unicode character data of n characters. n must be a value from 1 through 4,000.	String	Up to 4,000 Unicode characters
	nvarchar	Variable-length Unicode character data, n can be a value from 1 through 4,000.	String	Up to 4,000 Unicode characters
		N varchar (max) is not supported.		
Binary strings	binary	Fixed-length binary data with a length of n bytes, where n is a value from 1 through 8,000.	Bytes Writable. java	Up to 8,000 bytes

Data type category	SQL Server data type	SQL Server data type range	Sqoop data type	Sqoop data type range
	varbinary	Variable-length binary data. n can be a value from 1 through 8,000. Var binary(max) is not supported.	Bytes Writable. java	Up to 8,000 bytes

For a complete list of supported data types, please refer to the SQL Server-Hadoop Connector reference at `http://www.microsoft.com/en-us/download/confirmation.aspx?id=27584`.

Summary

Sqoop is a JDBC-based technology, which is used for bi-directional data transfers from Hadoop to any RDBMS solution. This opens up the scope to merge structured and unstructured data and provide powerful analytics on the data overall. The SQL Server-Hadoop Connector is a Sqoop implementation, which is specifically designed for data transfer between SQL Server and Hadoop. This chapter explained how to configure and install Sqoop on your Hadoop NameNode and execute sample `import/export` commands to move data to and from SQL Server and Hadoop. In the next chapter, you will learn to consume Hadoop data through another Apache supporting project called Hive. You would also learn how to use the client-side Hive ODBC driver to consume Hive data from Business Intelligence tools for example, SQL Server Integration Services.

3
Using the Hive ODBC Driver

Hive is a framework that sits on top of core Hadoop. It acts as a data warehousing system on top of HDFS and provides easy query mechanisms to the underlying HDFS data. Programming MapReduce jobs could be tedious and will have their own development, testing, and maintenance investments. Hive queries, called Hive Query Language (HQL) are broken down into MapReduce jobs under the hood and remain a complete abstraction to the user and provide a query-based access mechanism for Hadoop data. The simplicity and "SQL" – ness of the Hive queries have made it a popular and preferred choice for users, particularly, people familiar with traditional SQL skills love it since the ramp up time is much less. The following figure gives an overview of the Hive architecture:

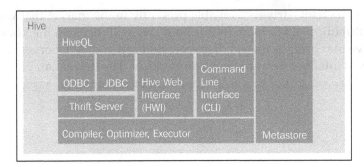

In effect, Hive enables you to create an interface layer over MapReduce that can be used in a similar fashion to a traditional relational database; enabling business users to use familiar tools such as Excel and SQL Server Reporting Services to consume data from Hadoop in a similar way as they would from a database system as SQL Server remotely through a ODBC connection. The rest of this chapter walks you through different Hive operations and using the Hive ODBC driver to consume the data.

After completing this chapter you will be able to:

- Download and install the Hive ODBC Driver
- Configure the driver to connect to Hive running on your Hadoop cluster on Linux
- Use **SQL Server Integration Services (SSIS)** to import data from Hive to SQL Server

The Hive ODBC Driver

One of the main advantages of Hive is that it provides a querying experience that is similar to that of a relational database, which is a familiar technique for many business users. Essentially, it allows all ODBC compliant clients to consume HDFS data through familiar **ODBC Data Sources (DSN)**, thus exposing Hadoop to a wide and diverse range of client applications.

There are several ODBC drivers available presently in the market that work on top of their own distribution of Hadoop. In this book, we will focus on the Microsoft ODBC driver for Hive that bridges the gap between Hadoop and SQL Server along with its rich business intelligence and visualization tools. The driver can be downloaded from `http://www.microsoft.com/en-us/download/details.aspx?id=37134`.

The driver comes in two flavors, 64 bit and 32 bit, so please make sure that you download and install the appropriate driver depending upon the bit configuration of your client application. In my case, since I am going to use the driver from 32 bit applications as Visual Studio, I have used the 32 bit flavor of the driver. Once, installation of the driver is complete, you can confirm the installation status by checking if you have the Hive ODBC driver present in the ODBC Data Administrator's list of drivers as shown in the following screenshot:

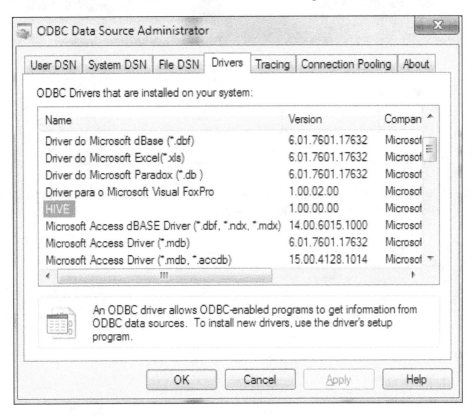

 In case you are on 64 bit Windows and you are using a 32 bit ODBC driver, you have to launch the ODBC Data Source Administrator from C:\Windows\SysWow64\odbcad32.exe.

Once the driver is installed successfully, perform the following steps to ensure that you can make a successful connection to Hive:

1. First, create a **System DSN**. In **ODBC Data Sources Administrator**, go to the **System DSN** tab and click on the **Add** Button as shown in the following screenshot:

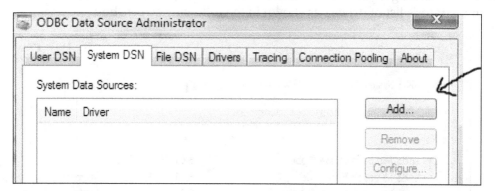

2. Choose, the **HIVE** driver in the next screen of the **Create New Data Source wizard** as shown in the following screenshot:

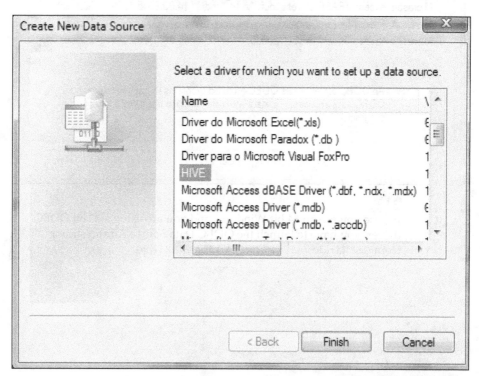

3. On clicking **Finish**, you are presented with the final **ODBC Hive Setup** screen. Enter the Hadoop cluster details as well as the credentials used to connect to the cluster. In this sample, I am using my Hadoop cluster deployed in Linux, RH2754741 is my NameNode:

4. Once created, a new **System DSN** should appear in the list as in the following screenshot. In this case, I have named my DSN as **HadoopOnLinux**.

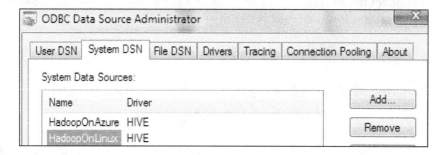

5. Now, we need to test the connection to Hive using the DSN **HadoopOnLinux**. The quickest way to test this out is to test from an .udl (**Universal Data Link**) file. To do this, create an empty .txt file and change the file extension to .udl. Then, double-click and open the .udl file, by default it should open with Microsoft OLE DB Core components and should look like the following screenshot:

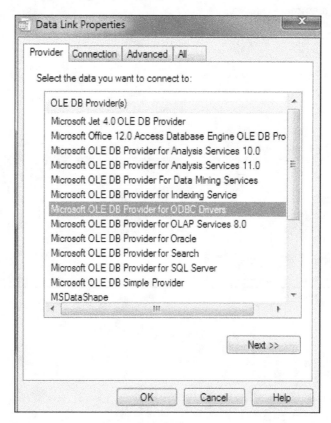

6. Choose **Microsoft OLE DB Provider for ODBC Drivers** and click on **Next**.

7. Choose the DSN **HadoopOnLinux** created in the previous steps. Provide the **User name** and **Password** for your Hadoop cluster and click on the **Test Connection** button. A successful test connection will confirm that the Hive ODBC driver is correctly set up as in the following screenshot and we are ready to go!

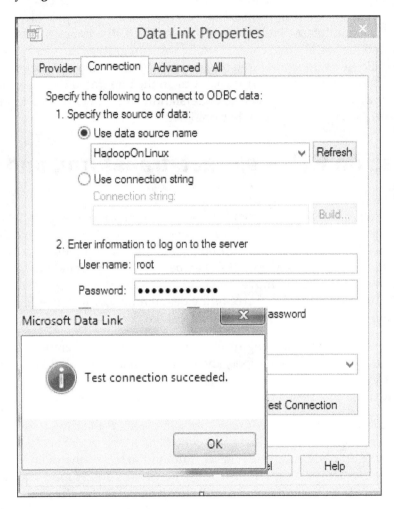

SQL Server Integration Services (SSIS)

Microsoft SQL Server is a complete suite of tools that include an RDBMS system, a multidimensional OLAP and tabular database engines, as well as other services, for example a broker service, a scheduling service (SQL Agent), and many more. As discussed in *Chapter 1, Introduction to Big Data and Hadoop*, it has become extremely important these days to integrate data between different sources. SQL Server also offers a powerful business intelligence stack, which provides rich features for data mining and interactive reporting. One of these BI components is an extract, transform, and load (ETL) tool called **SQL Server Integration Services (SSIS)**. SSIS offers the ability to merge structured and un-structured data by importing Hive data into SQL Server and apply powerful analytics on the integrated data. Throughout the rest of this chapter, we will get a basic understanding on how SSIS works and create a simple SSIS package to import data from Hive to SQL Server.

SSIS as an ETL – extract, transform, and load tool

The primary objective of an ETL tool is to be able to import and export data to and from heterogeneous data sources. This includes the ability to connect to external systems, as well as to transform or clean the data while moving the data between the external systems and the databases. SSIS can be used to import data to and from SQL Server. It can even be used to move data between external non-SQL systems without requiring SQL server to be the source or the destination. For instance, SSIS can be used to move data from an FTP server to a local flat file.

SSIS also provides a workflow engine for automation of the different tasks (for example, data flows, tasks executions, and so on.) that are executed in an ETL job. An SSIS package execution can itself be one step that is part of an SQL Agent job, and SQL Agent can run multiple jobs independent of each other.

An SSIS solution consists of one or more packages, each containing a control flow to perform a sequence of tasks. Tasks in a control flow can include calls to web services, FTP operations, file system tasks, automation of command line commands, and others. In particular, a control flow usually includes one or more data flow tasks, which encapsulate an in-memory, buffer-based pipeline of data from a source to a destination, with transformations applied to the data as it flows through the pipeline. An SSIS package has one control flow, and as many data flows as necessary. Data flow execution is dictated by the content of the control flow.

A detailed discussion on SSIS and its components are outside the scope of this book and it assumes that you are familiar with the basic SSIS package development using Business Intelligence Development Studio (SQL Server 2005/2008/2008 R2) or SQL Server Data Tools (SQL Server 2012). If you are a beginner in SSIS, it is highly recommended to read from a bunch of good SSIS books available as a prerequisite. In the rest of this chapter, we will focus on how to consume Hive data from SSIS using the Hive ODBC driver.

The prerequisites to develop the package shown in this chapter are SQL Server Data Tools, (which comes as a part of SQL Server 2012 Client Tools and Components) and the 32 bit Hive ODBC Driver installed. You will also need your Hadoop cluster up with Hive running on it.

Developing the package

SQL Server Data Tools (SSDT) is the integrated development environment available from Microsoft to design, deploy, and develop SSIS packages. SSDT is installed when you choose to install SQL Server Client tools and Workstation Components from your SQL Server installation media. SSDT supports creation of Integration Services, Analysis Services, and Reporting Services projects. Here, we will focus on Integration Services project type.

Creating the project

Perform the following steps for creating a new project.

1. Launch **SQL Server Data Tools** from **SQL Server 2012** program folders as shown in the following screenshot:

2. Create a new Project and choose **Integration Services Project** in the
New Project dialog as shown in the following screenshot:

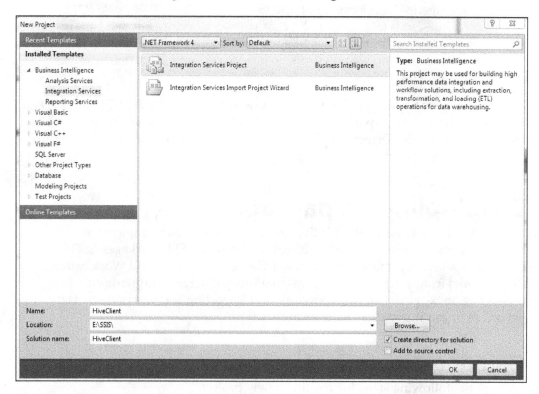

3. This should create the SSIS project with a blank `Package.dtsx` inside it
visible in the **Solution Explorer** window of the project as shown in the
following screenshot:

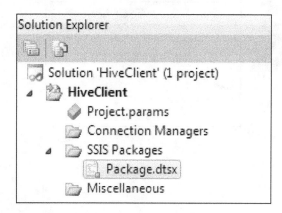

Creating the Data Flow

A Data Flow is a SSIS package component, which consists of the sources and destinations that extract and load data, the transformations that modify and extend data, and the paths that link sources, transformations, and destinations. Before you can add a data flow to a package, the package control flow must include a Data Flow task. The Data Flow task is the executable within the SSIS package, which creates, orders, and runs the data flow. A separate instance of the data flow engine is opened for each Data Flow task in a package. To create a Data Flow task, perform the following steps:

1. Double-click (or drag-and-drop) on a **Data Flow Task** from the toolbox on the left. This should place a **Data Flow Task** in the **Control Flow** canvas of the package as in the following screenshot:

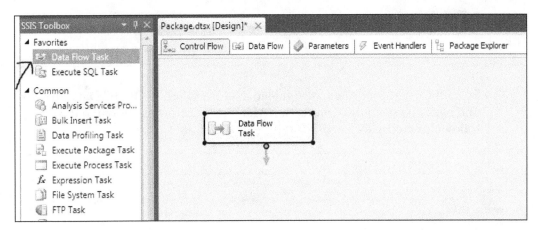

2. Double-click on the **Data Flow Task** or click on the **Data Flow** tab in SSDT to edit the task and design the source and destination components as in the following screenshot:

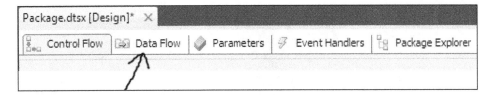

Creating the source Hive connection

The first thing we need to do is create a connection manager that will connect to our Hive data tables hosted in the Hadoop cluster. We will use an ADO.NET connection, which will use the DSN **HadoopOnLinux** we created earlier to connect to Hive. To create the connection, perform the following steps:

1. Right-click on the **Connection Managers** section in the project and click on **New ADO.Net Connection...** as shown in the following screenshot:

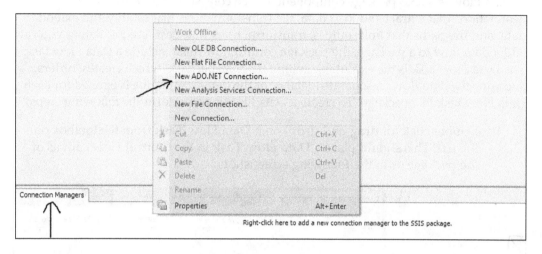

2. From the list of providers, navigate to **.Net Providers | ODBC Data Provider** and click on **OK** in the **Connection Manager** window as shown in the following screenshot:

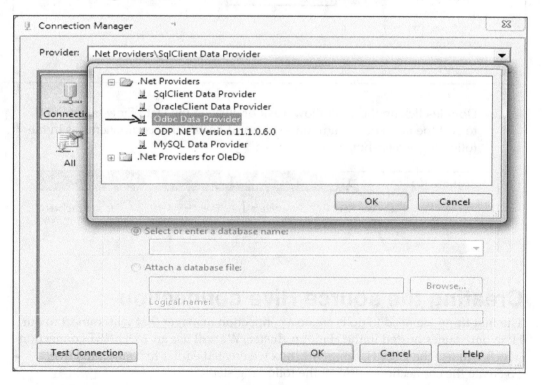

3. Select the **HadoopOnLinux** DSN from the Data Sources list. Provide the Hadoop cluster credentials and test connection should succeed as shown in the following screenshot:

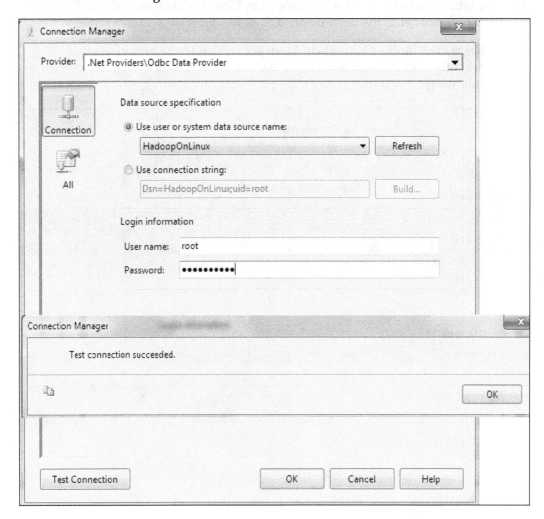

Creating the destination SQL connection

We will need to configure a connection to point to the SQL Server instance and the
database table, where we will import data from Hive. For this, we will need to create
a connection manager to the destination SQL as we did for the source Hive:

1. Right-click on the **Connection Manager** section of the project again,
   and this time, choose **New OLE DB Connection...** as shown in the
   following screenshot:

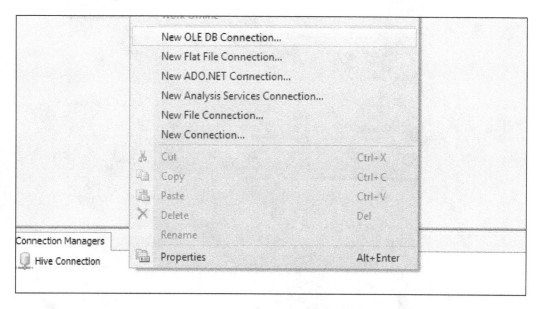

2. From the list of providers, choose **Native OLE DB | SQL Server Native Client 11.0**. Key in the target SQL Server name and select the database where the target table resides. Test connection should succeed confirming the validity of the connection manager for the destination as shown in the following screenshot:

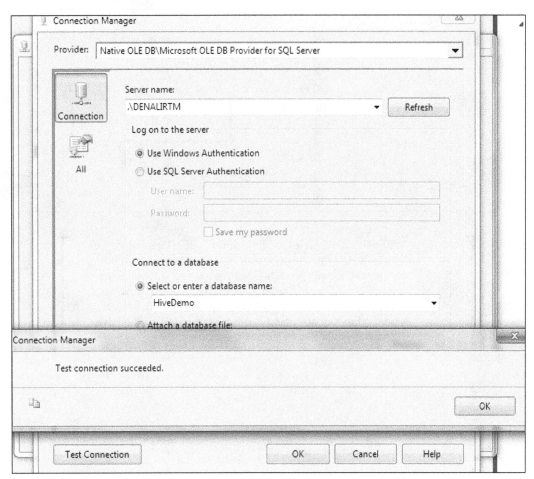

 In this example, I've chosen OLE DB to connect to SQL. You can also choose to use ADO.NET or an ODBC connection to do the same.

Creating the Hive source component

Next, we will need to configure a source component, which will connect to Hive and fetch the data. After the connection is successfully created, double-click to place an **ADO NET Source** on the Data Flow canvas as shown in the following screenshot:

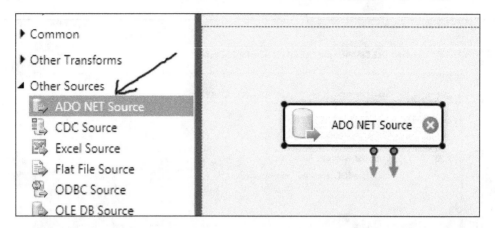

 With SSIS 2012, ODBC Source and ODBC Destination is a pair of Data Flow components that were included in the product. Though the ODBC Source component supports a lot of ODBC compliant data sources, as of this writing, this component does not support the Hive ODBC driver. Today, the only option to consume the Hive ODBC driver from SSIS is via the ADO.Net components.

Right-Click on the **ADO NET Source** and click on **Edit** to configure the source to connect to the Hive table using the connection just created. Select the connection manager (I named it **Hive Connection**) and the Hive table (In my case, it is the `facebookinsights` table). You can preview the data to ensure that the source can fetch the data without issues. Also, make sure, you navigate to the **Columns** tab and confirm that you can see all the columns from the table. Click on **OK** to complete the configuration as shown in following screenshot:

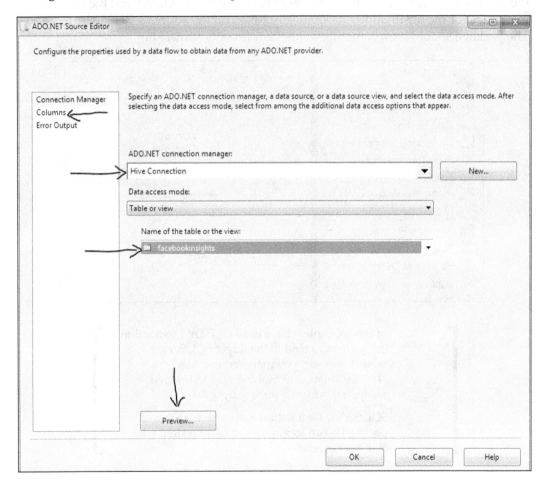

 You can also create the connection manager on the fly while configuring the source component by clicking on the **New** button adjacent to the **ADO.NET connection manager**.

Creating the SQL destination component

After the source is configured, we need to configure the destination where we want to import the Hive data. In this example, I am going to use SQL Server as the destination. To do this, double-click and place an **OLE DB Destination** component in the Data Flow canvas. Make sure, you connect the **ADO NET Source** and the **OLE DB Destination** components by dragging the arrow between the source and the destination. This is required for SSIS to generate the metadata and the column mappings for the destination automatically based on the source schema structure. The package should look something like the following screenshot:

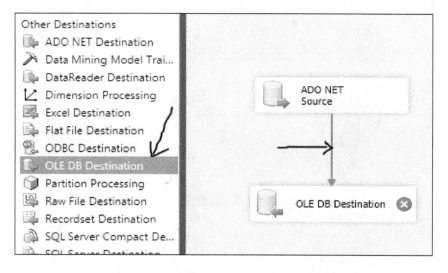

In this example, I have used OLE DB Destination component to bind to the target SQL Server table. However, you may also use ADO. NET Destination or SQL Server Destination components for the same purpose.

SQL Server Destination only works if the package is run locally on the same system where SQL Server resides.

Now, it is the time to configure the **OLE DB Destination** to point to the correct SQL connection and database table. To do this, right-click on the **OLE DB Destination** component and click on **Edit**. Select the **OLE DB connection manager** to SQL that we just created and the target table. In this case, I have named the connection as **SQL Connection** and I already have a predefined table created in the SQL database called `facebookinsights`. In case you don't have the table precreated, you can choose to create the destination table on the fly by clicking on the **New** button, adjacent to the **Name of the table or the view** drop-down. This is illustrated in the following screenshot:

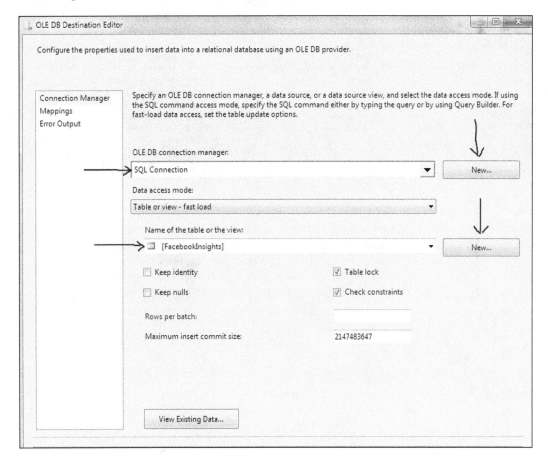

 You can also create the connection manager and the database table on the fly while configuring the destination component by clicking on the respective **New** buttons as shown in the previous screenshot.

Mapping the columns

Once this is done, make sure you navigate to the **Mappings** tab to ensure that the column mappings between the source and the destination is correct as shown in the following screenshot. Click on **OK** to complete the configuration.

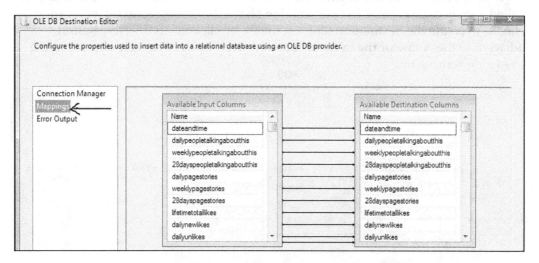

 If you choose to create the target table yourself and specify different column names than the source, you have to manually map each of these source and destination columns. SSIS's built-in column mapping intelligence is based on same column names, so in case they differ, make sure you set up the column mappings correctly.

The data flow between the source and destination along with the connection managers should like the following screenshot:

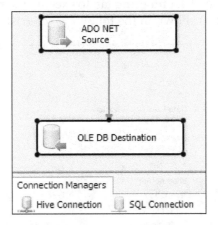

Running the package

Voila!! We are all set to go. From the menu bar, navigate to **Debug | Start Debugging** or press *F5* or click on the Play button in the toolbar to execute the package as shown in the following screenshot:

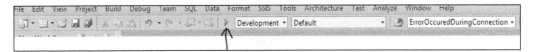

The package should run successfully, transfer records from the Hive table to the SQL Server table, and display the total number of records imported as shown in the following screenshot:

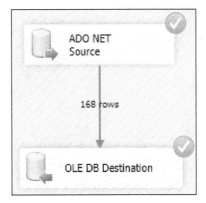

In case you are running this package in a 64 bit Windows Operating System, you will need to change the **Run64BitRuntime** property to **False** from the **Project** Properties | **Configuration** Properties | **Debugging** tab to execute the package as it is using the 32 bit Hive ODBC driver as shown in the following screenshot:

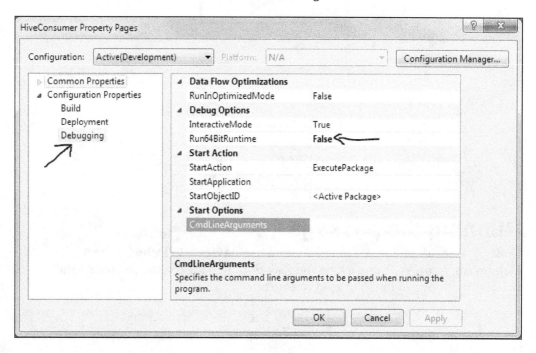

You can now schedule this package as a SQL Server job and run the data load on a periodic basis. You may also want to apply some transformation to the data before it loads into the target SQL warehouse to clean it or to apply necessary business logic using the built-in SSIS Data Flow Transformation components.

Summary

In this chapter, we had a dive into the Hadoop supporting project Hive. Hive acts as a data warehouse on top of HDFS providing easy, familiar SQL-like query structures called HQL to fetch the underlying data. HQLs are broken down into MapReduce code internally, thus relieving the end user from writing complex MapReduce code. We also learned about the Hive ODBC driver that acts as an interface between the client consumers and Hadoop; how to install the driver and how to test that the driver is successfully able to connect to Hive. We had a brief look into SQL Server and its business intelligence components as well in this chapter. We developed a sample package, which connects to Hive using the Hive ODBC driver and imports data from the Hive table `facebookinsights` to SQL Server. Once the data is in SQL Server, we can leverage warehousing solutions such as **SQL Server Analysis Services (SSAS)** to slice and dice the data as well as **SQL Server Reporting Services (SSRS)** for powerful reporting on the data. This also enables us to integrate non-relational data to be merged with traditional RDBMS data and extract information from it as a whole. In the next chapter, you will see how to use the Hive ODBC driver to create Linked Servers in SQL. You will also learn how to import data from Hive using linked server queries and create a Multidimensional model in SSAS for further processing.

4
Creating a Data Model with SQL Server Analysis Services

Apache Hadoop brings flexibility and scale to an extent which is not possible in the traditional RDBMS-based data warehousing systems for example, SQL Server. On top of the core Hadoop, Hive acts as a data warehouse to provide a logical schema over your HDFS data, which allows ad hoc query mechanisms to work with large datasets. However, query execution, performance, and turnaround times are often decisive factors for most common BI implementation scenarios. Query responses from Hadoop and Hive are predominantly batch operations, which are designed and expected to be time consuming and no-way close to real time. But there are scenarios that businesses demand, where they need real-time answers to their queries.

You could import data from Hadoop to SQL Server Analysis Services (SSAS) by using Hive Query Language (HQL). Analysis Services can then take it up from there and provide real-time insights and powerful reporting on the data. After completing this chapter, you should be able to:

- Create a SQL Linked Server to Hive
- Query the SQL Linked Server to fetch data from Hive
- Create Analysis Services Multidimensional Data Model from Hive

Configuring the SQL Linked Server to Hive

Since Hive tables are exposed only through ODBC, there is no direct way to connect an Analysis Services database to Hadoop as Analysis Services can only connect to OLE DB compliant data sources. To address this, the only way is to create a Linked Server in a SQL Server instance using Hive ODBC driver and consume it through OLE DB for ODBC. We will reuse the DSN **HadoopOnLinux** that we created during our earlier chapters to connect to Hive.

To create the Linked Server, perform the following steps:

1. Connect to the SQL Server instance using SQL Server Management Studio and expand the **Server Objects** as shown in the following screenshot:

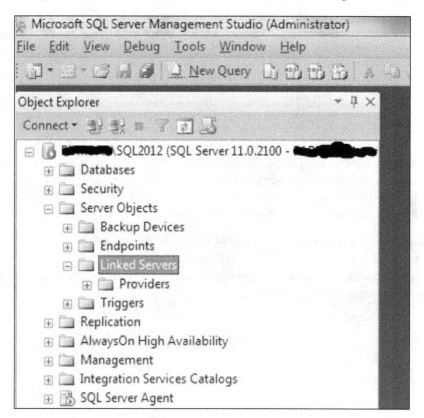

2. Right-click on **Linked Servers** and choose **New Linked Server**. This should bring up the **New Linked Server** window as shown in the following screenshot:

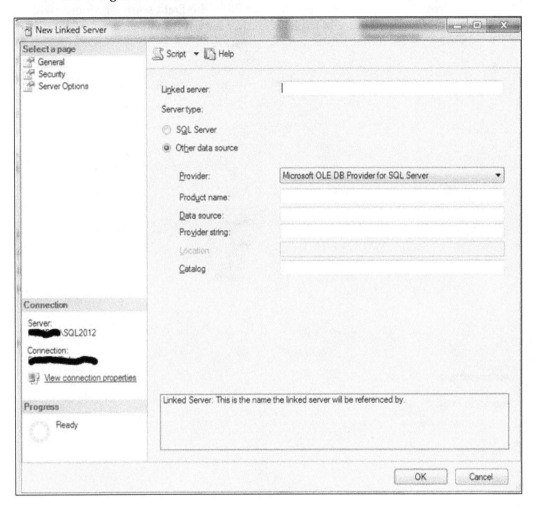

3. You have to fill in the details of the Hive Data source that you would like connect to. In this case, I have named the Linked Server as **LINKTOHIVE**. You have to choose **Microsoft OLE DB Provider for ODBC Drivers** from the **Provider** list. You will also have to fill in the **Data source** property with the DSN named **HadoopOnLinux** so that we have an appropriate **Provider string** as shown in the following screenshot:

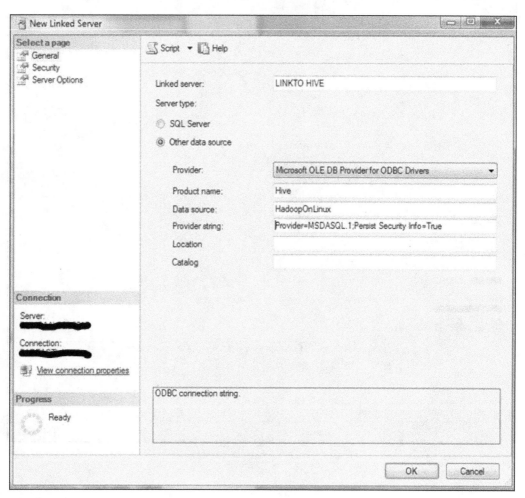

4. Navigate to the **Security** section, select **Be made using this security context** and provide your Hadoop cluster credentials as shown in the following screenshot:

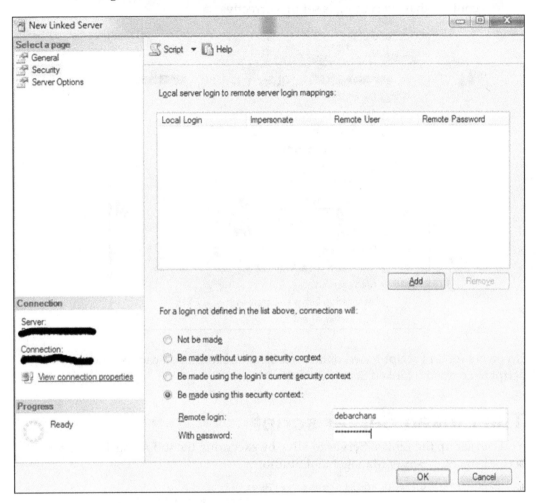

5. Click on **OK** and this should create a new Linked Server named **LINKTOHIVE** under **SQL Server Linked Servers** as shown in the following screenshot. You can right-click on the **Linked Server** and test connection to confirm that everything is set up correctly.

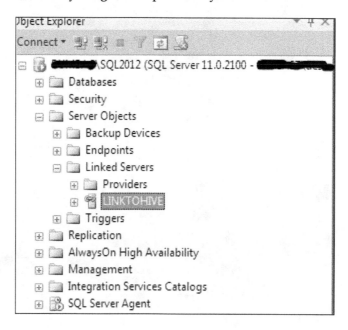

If you are fond of script-based database objects creation, you can use the following script to create the Linked Server as well:

The Linked Server script

You can set up the Linked Server to Hive by executing the following Transact-SQL script from SQL Server Management Studio:

```
EXECmaster.dbo.sp_addlinkedserver@server=
  N'LINKTOHIVE',@srvproduct=N'Hive',@provider=N'MSDASQL',
  @datasrc=N'HadoopOnLinux',@provstr=N'Provider=MSDASQL.1;
  Persist Security Info=True'
/* For security reasons the linked server remote logins password is
changed with ######## */
EXECmaster.dbo.sp_addlinkedsrvlogin@rmtsrvname=N'LINKTOHIVE',
  @useself=N'False',@locallogin=NULL,@rmtuser=N'debarchans',
  @rmtpassword='########'
```

> Make sure you replace the rmtuser and rmtpassword values with your own.

You can use the `OpenQuery` Transact-SQL command to connect to the data source, run the query on the Hadoop cluster, and return the results to SQL Server.

Using OpenQuery

The following Transact-SQL script illustrates how to query the `facebookinsights` Hive table we created earlier using the SQL Linked Server:

```
SELECT * FROM OpenQuery([LINKTOHIVE], 'SELECT * FROM
    facebookinsights;')
```

Executing this query from Query Analyzer should show us the records from the Hive table as shown in the following screenshot:

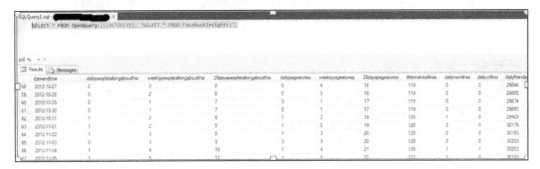

The next section of this chapter discusses creating a **Multidimensional Online Analytical Processing** data model (**MOLAP**) from the data imported by the Linked Server query. However, multidimensional projects only support SQL tables or views as their data sources. So prior to jumping on to the Business Intelligence project, we would create a view in our SQL database based on the Linked Server query.

Creating a view

The following Transact-SQL creates the view from the `OpenQuery` statement we used previously:

```
Create View KeyMetrices AS
    SELECT * FROM OpenQuery([LINKTOHIVE],'SELECT * FROM
    facebookinsights;')
```

 Analysis Services Tabular Project supports direct SQL queries to create data models.

Creating an SSAS data model

Once the Linked Server is created on the computer running SQL Server, it is pretty simple to connect Analysis Services to Hive in SQL Server Data Tools. The rest of this chapter will describe the way to import data from a Hive table into a SSAS Multidimensional and Data Mining Project using the view we created by following the steps as mentioned in the previous section.

Perform the following steps to create a SSAS data model:

1. In **SQL Server Data Tools**, on the **File** menu, click on **New**, and then click on **Project**. In the **New Project** dialog box, under **Installed Templates**, navigate to **Business Intelligence | Analysis Services**, and then select **Analysis Services Multidimensional and Data Mining Project** as shown in the following screenshot:

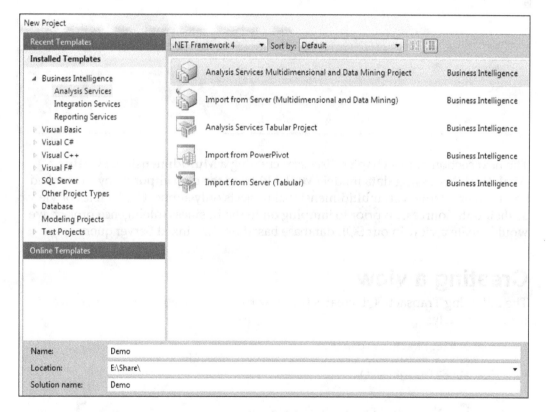

2. Here, you would need to specify the **Name** and the **Location** for your project files. By default, **Solution name** will be the same as the project name; however, if you want, you can type a different **Solution name**. I have named my project as **Demo**. Click on **OK** to proceed and create the project.

3. Once the project is created, the key tasks are to define your **Data Sources** and **Data Source Views**, which you can see in the **Solution Explorer** window as in the following screenshot:

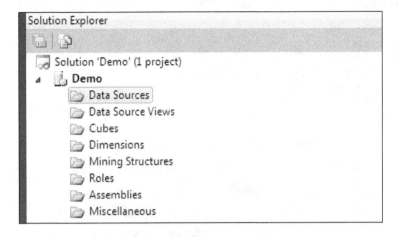

4. Right-click on **Data Sources** and choose **New Data Source**. This would launch the **Data Source Wizard** as in the following screenshot:

5. Next, you have to define the connection to the database where you created the Linked Server and the View. You could select the connection if it is already prepopulated in the **Data Source Wizard**, else, you could click on the **New** button to set up the connection as in the following screenshot:

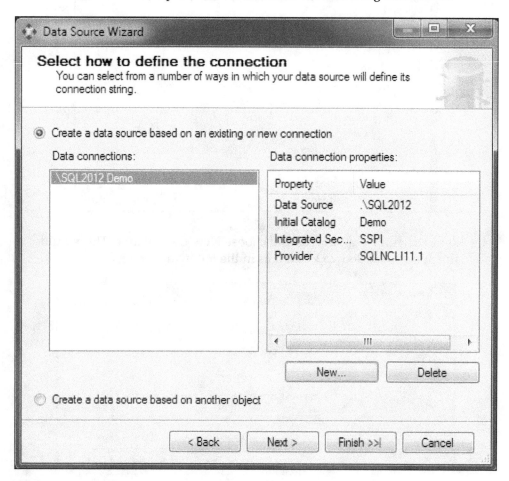

6. Next, in the **Impersonation Information** page, make sure that **Use the credentials of the current user** is selected as in the following screenshot:

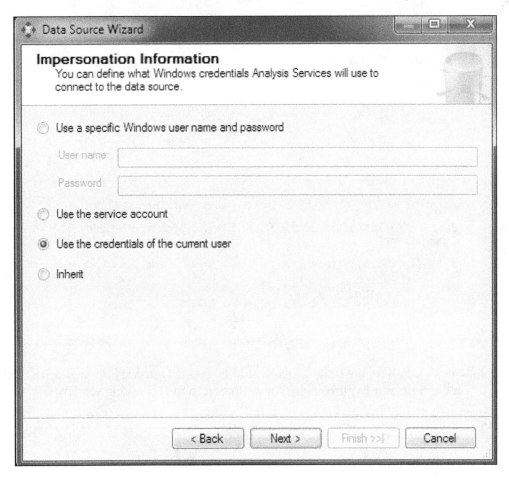

7. Click on **Next**, you could choose a **Data source name** for your connection as shown in the following screenshot:

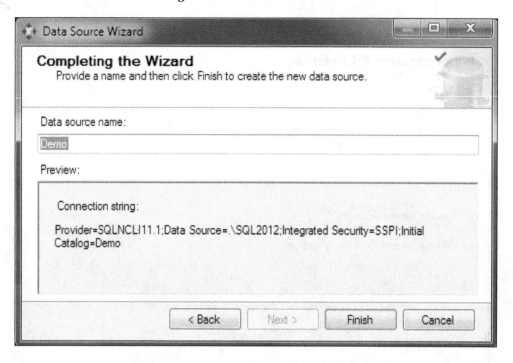

8. Click on **Finish**, the data source would be created successfully and displayed in the **Solution Explorer** window as shown in the following screenshot:

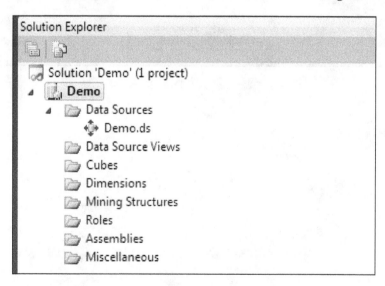

9. Once the data source is created, you would need to define the data source views. These views will actually serve as the models for further creation of relationships, cubes, and dimensions in your solution based on the requirements. To create a view, right-click on **Data Source Views** and choose **New** to launch the **Data Source View Wizard** as shown in the following screenshot:

10. Click on **Next** and select the data source **Demo** created previously, as shown in the following screenshot:

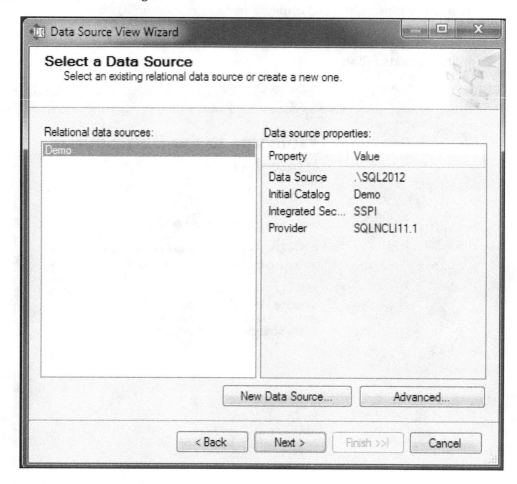

11. Click on **Next** and you should be able to see the **KeyMetrices** view we
    created in the previous section under the **Available objects** list. Click on
    the right arrow to move it under the **Included objects** list as shown in the
    following screenshot:

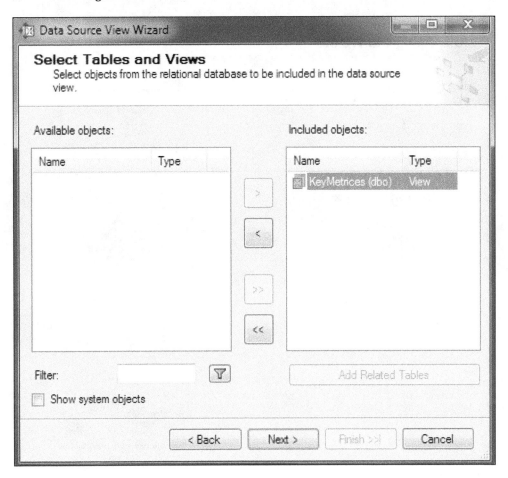

12. The last screen of the wizard is where you provide the name for your data source view and complete the wizard by clicking on **Finish** as in the following screenshot:

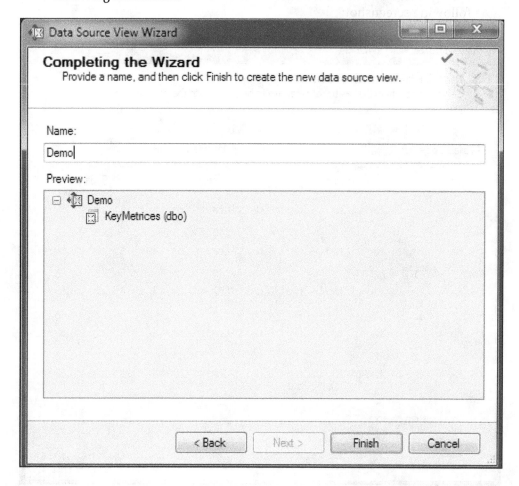

13. Clicking on **Finish** will create the view and fetch the columns from the **Key metrics$** view as shown in the following screenshot:

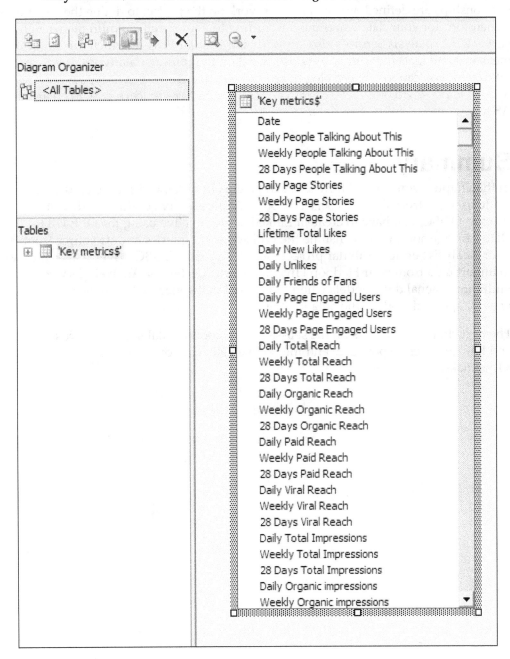

You can follow these steps as many times as required to add additional tables or views you may want to add into the model. Once the objects are imported and the relationships are defined, you can further work on the project to define the cubes and dimensions for your data warehouse according to your specific requirements. SQL Server 2012 Analysis Services also supports the Tabular Project, which can suggest measures and facts for your warehouse based on the column data types. If you are interested, you can follow the blog `http://dennyglee.com/2013/05/29/import-hadoop-data-into-sql-bi-semantic-model-tabular/` to learn how to create an AS tabular model from Hive data.

Summary

In this chapter, you learned how to leverage the Hive ODBC driver to consume Hadoop/Hive from Analysis Services. Since Analysis Services directly do not support ODBC, you have to create a Linked Server to Hive using the OLE DB to ODBC Bridge and in turn consume the Linked Server queries as data source from your Analysis Services Tabular project model. The Hive ODBC driver makes it easy to import data from your Hadoop Hive table into SQL Server Analysis Services multidimensional data models where Business Intelligence tools may be used to view, shape, and analyze the data further.

The next chapter will focus on the self-service BI tools available from Microsoft and how to generate powerful and interactive visualization using them with just a few clicks.

5
Using Microsoft's Self-Service Business Intelligence Tools

The focus of Business Intelligence is to empower business users with more accurate, reliable, and better information than they could obtain from operational systems. Traditional BI solutions have always relied on a centralized, cleansed, and transformed datastore that users can access through standardized reports and occasionally, an ad hoc query tool. Reports are developed by BI experts and the minimum requirement was to hire a set of professionals to run and maintain the infrastructure and the solutions.

After the deployment of such a system, requests for a catered data source for a specific need or a new data source could take days to be served as it has to go through the defined change management requests. Since only a few resources are trained well enough to handle these requests, the changes may even take weeks to implement.

Many executives have realized that the current BI approach is unable to keep pace with the inflow of data in a dynamic business environment. Data is everywhere now, and growing exponentially. Relying too much on a big-budget BI team for everything is no longer acceptable. This has led to the dawn of a new technology called self-service BI. Self-service BI is the talk of the town at the moment. It allows you to perform a professional level of data analysis quickly and efficiently without the need to hire an expensive set of BI infrastructure or a team of skilled individuals. Microsoft provides a set of rich self-service BI tools that can connect to a wide variety of data sources including SQL Server 2012 and Hadoop and quickly provide insights on the data. It combines with powerful reporting facilities and produces a seamless, interactive visualization on the underlying data. This is often at the top of the management pyramid where business executives review these reports and take decisions for betterment of the business and more efficient resource utilization. In this chapter you will learn about:

- Microsoft self-service BI tools
- Using PowerPivot to generate a data model
- Using Power View to create interactive report on the data model

PowerPivot enhancements

SQL Server 2012 brings in enhanced data analysis capabilities for both PowerPivot client in the form of the Excel add-in as well as the PowerPivot server-side component in SharePoint. This enables Microsoft Office users to have self-service business intelligence capabilities with merely a few clicks, something which was never there before. Users are now able to integrate data from heterogeneous sources more easily and provide powerful visualization on the data using familiar tools such as Excel and SharePoint, thus enabling the businesses to take correct decisions.

PowerPivot is offered as an add-in to Excel 2010 that allows data integration from any source and syndication, including **Open Data Protocol (ODATA)** feeds, RDBMS sources, Hadoop, and so on. Using PowerPivot, you could create your own data models from any of the diverse data sources previously mentioned and import large amounts of data into Excel directly. If there is a need to have these data models as a shared repository, they can be published in SharePoint server and shared across the enterprise very easily. The PowerPivot models can also serve as data sources for other business intelligence tools available in the market including Power View (discussed later in this chapter) to generate intuitive and interactive reports for trend analysis, predictive analysis, and so on.

The following section explains how to generate a PowerPivot data model based on the `facebookinsights` Hive table created earlier using the Hive ODBC driver. We have used Excel 2013 for the demos. Make sure you turn on the required add-ins for Excel as shown in the following screenshot to build the samples used throughout this chapter:

1. Navigate to **File | Options | Add-ins**. In the **Manage** drop-down list, choose **COM Add-ins** and click on **Go**, and enable the following add-ins:

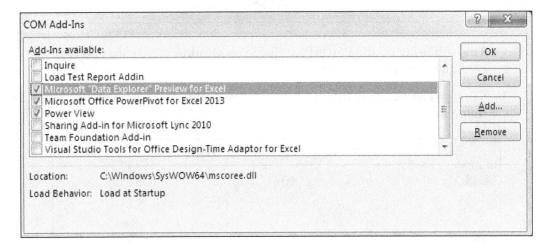

 PowerPivot is also supported in Excel 2010. Power View and Data Explorer are available only in Excel 2013.

2. To create a PowerPivot model, open Excel, navigate to the **PowerPivot** ribbon and click on **Manage** as shown in the following screenshot:

This will bring up the PowerPivot for Excel window where we need to configure the connection to Hive.

3. Click on **Get External Data** and choose **From other Sources** as shown in the following screenshot:

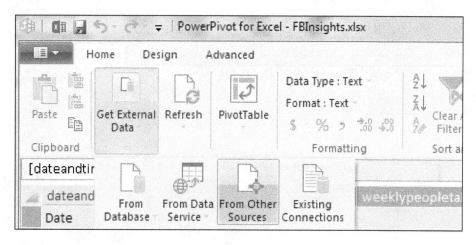

4. Since we would be using the Hive ODBC provider, choose **Others (OLEDB/ODBC)** and click on **Next** on the **Table Import Wizard** as shown in the following screenshot:

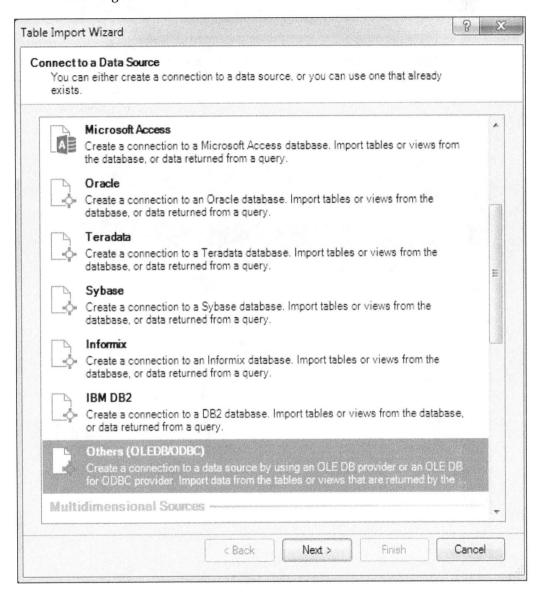

5. The next screen in the wizard accepts the connection string for our data source. It is easier to build the connection string instead of writing it manually. So, click on the **Build** button to bring up the **Data Link** window where you can select the **HadooponLinux** DSN we created earlier, and provide the correct credentials to access the Hadoop cluster. Make sure to check **Allow saving password** so that the password is retained in the underlying PowerPivot **Table Import Wizard**. Also, verify that test connection succeeds as shown in the following screenshot:

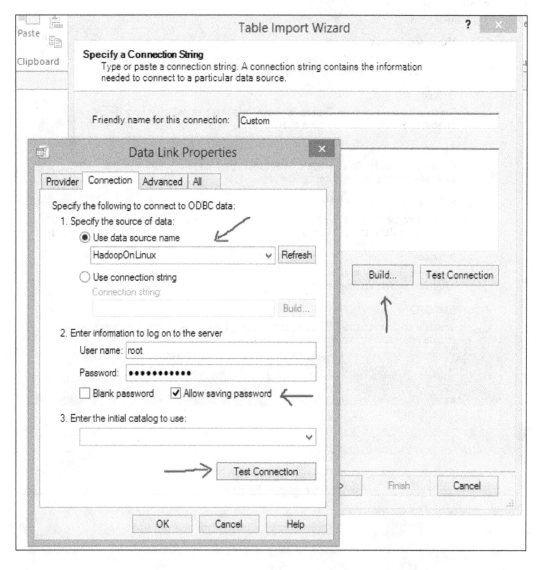

6. The **Table Import Wizard** dialogue should now be populated with the appropriate **Connection String** as shown below in the following screenshot:

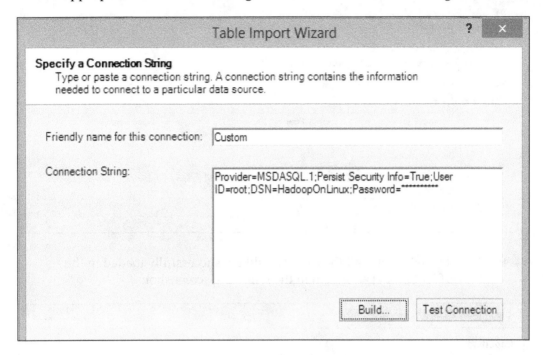

7. Next, we are going to choose the Hive table directly, but we can also write a query (HiveQL) to fetch the data as shown in the following screenshot:

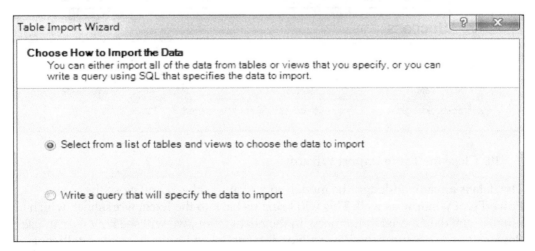

8. Select the `facebookinsights` table and click on **Finish** to complete the configuration as in the following screenshot:

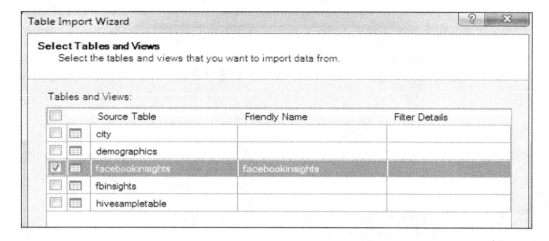

9. The Hive table with all the rows should get successfully loaded in the PowerPivot model as shown in the following screenshot:

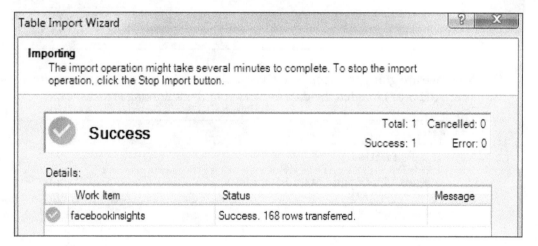

10. Close the **Table Import Wizard**.

The data is already added in the model, so we can go ahead and close the PowerPivot window as well. This will bring us back to the Excel worksheet, which now has the data model in-memory. In the next section, we will see how we can use Power View to consume the PowerPivot data model and quickly create intelligent and interactive reports.

Power View for Excel

Microsoft Excel 2013 introduces a brand new self-service BI tool called Power View. This is also a part of Microsoft SharePoint 2013 included with SQL Server 2012 Reporting Services Service Pack 1 Add-in for Microsoft SharePoint Server 2013 Enterprise Edition. Both of the client side (Excel) and server side (SharePoint) implementations of Power View offer an interactive way to explore and visualize your data as well as to generate interactive reports on top of the underlying data.

The rest of this chapter shows a sample Power View report based on the facebookinsights table's data to give you a quick idea about the powerful reporting features from the surface level. The details on 'How to design a Power View report' as well as Power View integration with SharePoint is outside the scope of this book and are not discussed in depth.

> Power View is only supported in Excel 2013. You need to install the Power View add-in for Excel.

To create a Power View report based on the PowerPivot data model created earlier, click on the **Insert** ribbon in Excel and click on **Power View** as shown in the following screenshot:

This should launch a new Power View window with the PowerPivot model already available to it as shown in the following screenshot:

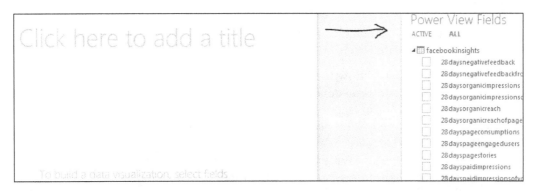

We can select the fields we require and display it in our report. There are options to choose between different types of charts, tabular and matrix reports. As an example, I've created a report which shows the number of likes and fans for my Facebook page over a period of time as shown in the following screenshot:

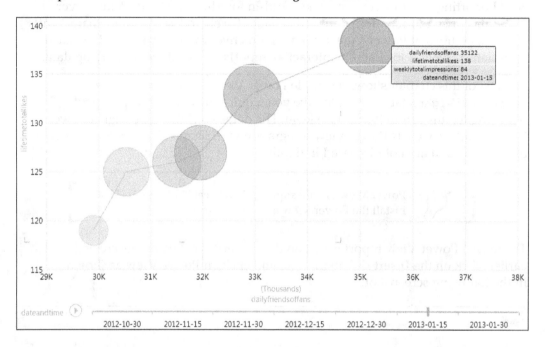

The Power View designer gives you different types of chart, axis, and timeline layouts, which make it really easy to generate a simple visualization. However, these self-service tools should not be thought as replacements to our existing BI solutions. It is not a replacement for standard parameterized reports, but an augmentation to enable key functions and leaders to leverage their own analytics, without pressuring scarce IT resources.

Summary

In this chapter, we learned how to integrate Microsoft self-service BI tools with Hadoop and Hive to consume data and generate powerful visualizations on the data. With the paradigm shifts in technology, the industry is trending towards an era where Information Technology will be a consumer product. An individual should be able to visualize the insights he needs to an extent from a client side add-in like Power View. These self-service BI tools provide the capability of connecting and talking to a wide variety of data sources seamlessly and create in-memory data models combining the data from these diverse sources for powerful reporting.

Index

Sqoop import tool
  about 19, 23, 24
  data types 24, 26
  tables, importing in Hive 22
sqoop job command 16
sqoop version command 16
SSAS data model
  creating 60-70
SSDT 37
SSIS
  about 36
  as ETL tool 36
SSIS packages
  developing 37
  running 49, 50
SSIS packages development
  columns, mapping 48, 49
  Data Flow, creating 39
  destination SQL connection, creating 42, 43
  Hive source component, creating 44, 45
  project, creating 37, 38
  source Hive connection, creating 39, 41
  SQL destination component, creating 46, 47
SSRS 30

T

Table Import Wizard 76
TaskTracker 11, 12

W

world data 7

Thank you for buying
Microsoft SQL Server 2012 with Hadoop

About Packt Publishing

Packt, pronounced 'packed', published its first book "Mastering phpMyAdmin for Effective MySQL Management" in April 2004 and subsequently continued to specialize in publishing highly focused books on specific technologies and solutions.

Our books and publications share the experiences of your fellow IT professionals in adapting and customizing today's systems, applications, and frameworks. Our solution based books give you the knowledge and power to customize the software and technologies you're using to get the job done. Packt books are more specific and less general than the IT books you have seen in the past. Our unique business model allows us to bring you more focused information, giving you more of what you need to know, and less of what you don't.

Packt is a modern, yet unique publishing company, which focuses on producing quality, cutting-edge books for communities of developers, administrators, and newbies alike. For more information, please visit our website: www.packtpub.com.

About Packt Enterprise

In 2010, Packt launched two new brands, Packt Enterprise and Packt Open Source, in order to continue its focus on specialization. This book is part of the Packt Enterprise brand, home to books published on enterprise software – software created by major vendors, including (but not limited to) IBM, Microsoft and Oracle, often for use in other corporations. Its titles will offer information relevant to a range of users of this software, including administrators, developers, architects, and end users.

Writing for Packt

We welcome all inquiries from people who are interested in authoring. Book proposals should be sent to author@packtpub.com. If your book idea is still at an early stage and you would like to discuss it first before writing a formal book proposal, contact us; one of our commissioning editors will get in touch with you.

We're not just looking for published authors; if you have strong technical skills but no writing experience, our experienced editors can help you develop a writing career, or simply get some additional reward for your expertise.

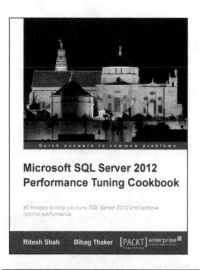

Microsoft SQL Server 2012
Performance Tuning Cookbook

80 recipes to help you tune SQL Server 2012 and achieve optimal performance

Ritesh Shah   Bihag Thaker

Microsoft SQL Server 2012 Performance Tuning Cookbook

ISBN: 978-1-84968-574-0   Paperback: 478 pages

80 recipes to help you tune SQL Server 2012 and achieve optimal performance

1. Learn about the performance tuning needs for SQL Server 2012 with this book and ebook

2. Diagnose problems when they arise and employ tricks to prevent them

3. Explore various aspects that affect performance by following the clear recipes

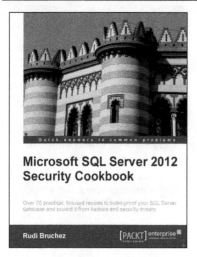

Microsoft SQL Server 2012
Security Cookbook

Over 70 practical, focused recipes to bullet-proof your SQL Server database and protect it from hackers and security threats

Rudi Bruchez

Microsoft SQL Server 2012 Security Cookbook

ISBN: 978-1-84968-588-7   Paperback: 322 pages

Over 70 practical, focused recipes to bullet-proof your SQL Server database and protect it from hackers and security threats

1. Practical, focused recipes for securing your SQL Server database

2. Master the latest techniques for data and code encryption, user authentication and authorization, protection against brute force attacks, denial-of-service attacks, and SQL Injection, and more

3. A learn-by-example recipe-based approach that focuses on key concepts to provide the foundation to solve real world problems

Please check **www.PacktPub.com** for information on our titles

Hadoop MapReduce Cookbook

ISBN: 978-1-84951-728-7   Paperback: 300 pages

Recipes for analyzing large and complex datasets with Hadoop MapReduce

1. Learn to process large and complex data sets, starting simply, then diving in deep

2. Solve complex big data problems such as classifications, finding relationships, online marketing and recommendations

3. More than 50 Hadoop MapReduce recipes, presented in a simple and straightforward manner, with step-by-step instructions and real world examples

Hadoop Beginner's Guide

ISBN: 978-1-84951-730-0   Paperback: 398 pages

Learn how to crunch big data to extract meaning from the data avalanche

1. Learn tools and techniques that let you approach big data with relish and not fear

2. Shows how to build a complete infrastructure to handle your needs as your data grows

3. Hands-on examples in each chapter give the big picture while also giving direct experience

Please check **www.PacktPub.com** for information on our titles

* 9 7 8 1 7 8 2 1 7 7 9 8 2 *